The
Set Boundaries
Workbook

The Set Boundaries Workbook

Practical Exercises for Understanding Your Needs and Setting Healthy Limits

Nedra Glover Tawwab, MSW, LCSW

A TarcherPerigee Book

tarcherperigee

TarcherPerigee
an imprint of Penguin Random House LLC
penguinrandomhouse.com

TarcherPerigee with tp colophon is a registered trademark of Penguin Random House LLC

Most TarcherPerigee books are available at special quantity discounts for bulk purchase for sales promotions, premiums, fund-raising, and educational needs. Special books or book excerpts also can be created to fit specific needs. For details, write: SpecialMarkets@penguinrandomhouse.com.

ISBN 9780593421482
ebook ISBN 9780593421499

Printed in the United States of America
12th Printing

Book design by Silverglass

Contents

Author's Note

"Is therapy for everyone?" We may not all have access to therapy, or the resources or the desire to go, but we can all benefit from the insights discovered through therapy. In 2017, when I started using Instagram to share information about relationships, mental health, and healthy living, I did so to make the tools for healing and for growing more accessible.

Like therapy itself, therapeutic tools can also be helpful. This book is such a tool, and you can use it on your own or in conjunction with a licensed professional. At any time while reading this book, if the content feels too heavy, please pause. If you can't shake the heaviness, take it as a sign to seek therapy, as you may need more support.

Introduction

Because I'm a therapist, people often assume I've mastered setting boundaries. I haven't. We can't master something that's a continual practice. I cannot master brushing my teeth, for example. It will be something I do over and over, day after day. I have gotten better at brushing my teeth, and you can get better at practicing boundaries. With practice, you will get better at noticing when they are needed and at executing them.

In my first book, *Set Boundaries, Find Peace: A Guide to Reclaiming Yourself*, I shared my expertise based on fourteen years as a therapist and what I know about boundaries. The book is filled with information about what you need to know. We can *know better* and not do better, however, because it can be hard or seem impossible to change. This workbook will help you apply what you know to make real, positive changes.

I've always known when things didn't feel right. I knew that something was wrong in my relationships, but whenever I tried to fix it, I'd receive pushback, belittling, or shaming. How dare I want something different?

In college, when it became paramount for me to implement limitations with others, I had no words for what I was trying to do. With the help of a therapist, I discovered that I was setting boundaries. She reassured me that it was a healthy thing to do.

It's daring to live a boundaried life.

It's brave to run the risk of others becoming upset with you.

It takes courage to use your voice.

Even through fear, you can set boundaries.

Even through guilt, you can set boundaries.

This workbook is intended to help you:

- Practice setting limits and expectations in your relationship with yourself and others.
- Work through your feelings of discomfort and guilt about setting and maintaining boundaries.
- Understand what prevents you from advocating for yourself with others.
- Improve the way you communicate your boundaries.
- Integrate boundaries as a continuous way of being.

The Set Boundaries Workbook is intended to be a continual resource. Even after you've completed this book, you will need to practice setting and maintaining boundaries. When you struggle to set a new boundary or want to refresh your skills, come back to this book.

The Need for Practice

I love talking to people, and it's my job to listen. But it's when my clients and people in my community begin to act on what we've talked about that real change occurs. Likewise, when we read, we may increase our knowledge, but knowledge is of little use unless we put it into practice. For your life to change, it's important to apply what you know. Practice does not make perfect, but it will make you better. Toward that end, this workbook is an application manual.

In keynotes and workshops about boundaries, I like to leave people with the ability to start the work today. Each time you open this workbook, you can practice using its tools in your daily life.

There is no hurry, of course. Each of us changes in our own time. But the longer you go without acting, the longer you sit with the discomfort of unhealthy boundaries.

Before I had healthy boundaries, I would:

- Wait for people to figure out what I needed
- Allow people to borrow money that I couldn't afford to loan
- Easily say yes to things I didn't have time to do
- Spend money without considering my finances
- Allow people to borrow items and not return them
- Offer to help in cases where I did not have the capacity
- Do what people wanted without considering my needs
- Tell people what was best for them
- Make myself available to people when I didn't have the time
- Often feel resentful toward people for asking me to help and then mad at myself for feeling that way

How to Use This Book

Reflection

Take the time to consider what is said. Let the words sit with you. Allow them to penetrate your memories, both positive and negative. Don't avoid the urge to feel what your body needs to move through this book. Pause and take a breath, if necessary, but come back. Don't abandon your healing.

Journaling

Journaling is an important step in processing your thoughts. It can be done with pen and paper (my preference), in the note section on your phone, using a diary app, in a document on your computer, or via audio or video recordings. Try a few methods to see what works best for you. Comfort is vital for consistent journaling. You must find your unique rhythm. Throughout this book, if you find yourself feeling uncomfortable, journal through it. At the end of each chapter, space is provided for you to write through your feelings about the text and exercises you completed.

Note: If your trust in journaling has been violated (e.g., someone has read your journal without your permission), consider using your phone or computer and locking the document. Despite your concerns about being violated, it's healthy to get your feelings out and a vital part of healing.

Checklists

The checklists in this workbook will help you gauge where you are and how to move forward. Use them as a measure to learn more about yourself. Choose whichever answer comes to you first so that you can move through the checklists without focusing too long on one answer. This book is meant to help you grow, not to make you overthink.

Pause and Gather Yourself

In each chapter you will see a reminder to pause. Take that time to step away from the material and give yourself a moment to regenerate. At the end of each chapter you will be reminded to gather yourself. Allow yourself to rest and reflect, and write down any thoughts you have. Also, at any point, take a break when one is needed.

Exercises

Complete the exercises when you have at least fifteen minutes to process the work being asked of you. Each exercise will help you deepen your understanding of the material. Remember, knowledge and application are equally important.

Some of the exercises will require you to practice something in the present, while others will help you shift through patterns from the past that have led to where you are now.

Important Reminders

Throughout this book you will see reminders intended to help you gain a deeper understanding of the material.

Find Support

Everyone has boundaries, even if they don't recognize them. As you are working through this book, talk to a friend, partner, or family member who can support you in this work. Please read some of the comments under one of my social media posts on boundaries. There are so many who, like you, are learning and applying this information. Community is so important in our growth and healing.

Take a moment to reflect and journal about your deepest fears for starting or continuing your journey of building boundaries:

_____

_____

_____

_____

_____

_____

_____

If I had healthier boundaries, my life would be different in the following ways:

_____

_____

_____

_____

_____

_____

_____

I have used the following as barriers to setting boundaries:

_____

_____

_____

_____

_____

_____

_____

_____

_____

_____

_____

Sometimes, our mindset is the biggest barrier. Believing we can't is what keeps us from trying and succeeding in our efforts. This workbook will help you overcome the mindset of "can't." In any relationship and with yourself, you can exercise boundaries. Even with the most difficult people, there are ways to exercise boundaries.

1

What Does It Mean to Have Healthy Boundaries?

When I told people I was writing a book about boundaries, one said, "You're writing a book about cutting people off?"

Another person said, "I have great boundaries: I know how to say no."

Having healthy boundaries could mean saying no and cutting people off. But that's only scratching the surface.

EXERCISE

To better understand what you think about boundaries, use the diagram on the next page to explore what they mean to you. It's important to know what language and behaviors you use to describe them.

A Working Definition of "Boundaries"

Boundaries are ways to communicate our needs to others via words and actions. They are also perimeters that we establish with ourselves and others. Therefore, boundaries aren't just about telling other people what to do but are also about holding yourself accountable for creating your life.

Your Definition
of Boundaries

Boundaries are expectations and needs that help you feel safe and comfortable in your relationships. Expectations in relationships help you stay mentally and emotionally well. An essential part of feeling comfortable in interactions with others is also learning when to say no or yes.

In society, we live with lots of boundaries and rules of engagement. For example, traffic lights are boundaries that control the flow of traffic and keep drivers safe. We all have plenty of practice adhering to boundaries; even the people with whom you have the most difficult time setting boundaries have experience obeying rules.

CHECKLIST

It's important to know the signs that you are suffering from unhealthy boundaries, and it's important to react before you lose your peace or find yourself in crisis. Check the signs that apply to you at this time:

- ❏ Neglecting self-care
- ❏ Feeling overwhelmed
- ❏ Desire to run away from your responsibilities
- ❏ Resentment
- ❏ Avoiding interactions with others
- ❏ Burnout
- ❏ Always the helper, never the one being helped
- ❏ Inability to say no
- ❏ Unable to ask for help
- ❏ Difficulty allowing others to help you
- ❏ Doing things with no support
- ❏ Rescuing others
- ❏ Loaning money or possessions

Why Is It Important to Have Healthy Boundaries?

Anxiety, depression, and burnout, among other issues, can result from your inability to set healthy expectations with yourself and others. Your body and mind know when you've had too much. Unfortunately, it's common for people to fight against the signs that limitations are needed.

We can't do it all, and we shouldn't try.

We can't be everything to everyone, and we shouldn't try.

We can't please everyone, and we shouldn't try.

How Do I Know If I Have Unhealthy Boundaries?

Pay attention to your feelings. Do you regularly ignore the desire in your head to say no? It's time to start listening to that desire.

FILL IN THE BLANKS BELOW

To gain a deeper understanding of how feelings are key in determining your need for boundaries, complete the following statements:

I fear setting a boundary with _____ about _____
_____ .

I assume they will react in the following way: _____
_____ .

When I interact with _____ , I feel anxious.
_____ .

I become frustrated when _____ does _____
_____ .

I would feel better if they _____
_____ .

It would be helpful if I set the following boundary: _____
_____ .

When I see a text from _____ , I feel _____
_____ .

This might be an indication that _____
_____ .

Unhealthy Boundaries (Porous and Rigid)

There are two unhealthy ways people place boundaries.

Type 1: Porous Boundaries

Porous boundaries are weak or poorly expressed, and they are unintentionally harmful to you. They lead to feeling depleted, overextending yourself, depression, anxiety, and unhealthy relationship dynamics. Porous boundaries are often the cause of enmeshment (lacking emotional separation between you and another person), codependency (unhealthy closeness), and people-pleasing.

Examples of porous boundaries (enmeshment):
- Spending no time apart
- Entangling other people's emotions and thoughts with your own (no separation)
- Sharing everything because it's expected
- Seeing differences as a threat
- Agreeing with everything
- Believing it's your job to fix other people
- Maintaining all the same thoughts and values
- Never making decisions without including others
- Being unable to say no
- Supporting unhealthy habits that keep people dependent

People are not able to exist without help from others. Needing people is not codependence. Enmeshing with them and losing who you are is codependence. Making it your job to rescue them from problems of their own doing (without being asked) is codependence. Losing touch with your needs and taking on someone else's is codependence. Mutual closeness is healthy, but entangling who you are and how you feel based on someone else is not healthy.

Type 2: Rigid Boundaries (Strict Rules)
Rigid boundaries involve building walls to keep others out as a way to keep yourself safe. But staying safe by locking yourself in is also unhealthy and leads to a whole other set of problems.

Rigid boundaries are a self-protective mechanism meant to build distance.

This typically comes from a fear of vulnerability or a history of being taken advantage of. People with rigid boundaries don't allow exceptions to their stringent rules even when it would be healthy for them.

Rigid boundaries lead to counter-dependency, where we start to believe that we don't need anyone. Think "the strong one" who believes that they can handle everything without help.

CHECKLIST
Use the lists below to check off signs that your boundaries are either porous or rigid.

Porous
- ❑ Oversharing
- ❑ Codependency
- ❑ Enmeshment
- ❑ Inability to say no
- ❑ People-pleasing
- ❑ Dependency on feedback from others
- ❑ Paralyzing fear of being rejected
- ❑ Accepting mistreatment

Rigid
- ❑ Never sharing
- ❑ Building walls
- ❑ Avoiding vulnerability
- ❑ Cutting people out
- ❑ Having high expectations of others
- ❑ Enforcing strict rules

When your boundaries feel unhealthy, do they tend to be porous or rigid?

Healthy Boundaries

When your boundaries are healthy, you are clear about your needs, you say no when needed, you respect other people's boundaries, and you share yourself in ways that feel comfortable to you.

Healthy boundaries in one relationship don't mean healthy boundaries across relationships.

You can be excellent at setting boundaries at work and with your friends but struggle with setting boundaries with your parents. For example, your fears and how people have made you feel comfortable or uncomfortable in a relationship may determine the level of difficulty you have in setting boundaries in certain areas.

Pause: At any point while going through these exercises, take a moment to stop and be mindful of your breath. Focus your attention on breathing in deeply through your nose and out through your mouth.

EXERCISE

Please circle the type of boundaries most present for you in each of these relationships.

Parent	Porous	Rigid	Healthy
Parent	Porous	Rigid	Healthy
Parent figure	Porous	Rigid	Healthy
Parent figure	Porous	Rigid	Healthy
Sibling _____	Porous	Rigid	Healthy
Sibling _____	Porous	Rigid	Healthy
Sibling _____	Porous	Rigid	Healthy

Sibling _____	Porous	Rigid	Healthy
Family _____	Porous	Rigid	Healthy
Family _____	Porous	Rigid	Healthy
Partner	Porous	Rigid	Healthy
Friend _____	Porous	Rigid	Healthy
Friend _____	Porous	Rigid	Healthy
Friend _____	Porous	Rigid	Healthy
Friend _____	Porous	Rigid	Healthy
Friend _____	Porous	Rigid	Healthy
Work roles	Porous	Rigid	Healthy
Coworker _____	Porous	Rigid	Healthy
Coworker _____	Porous	Rigid	Healthy
Coworker _____	Porous	Rigid	Healthy
Boss	Porous	Rigid	Healthy
Social media and technology	Porous	Rigid	Healthy
Finances	Porous	Rigid	Healthy
Mental health	Porous	Rigid	Healthy
Physical health	Porous	Rigid	Healthy
Other _____	Porous	Rigid	Healthy
Other _____	Porous	Rigid	Healthy
Other _____	Porous	Rigid	Healthy

Gather Yourself

What came up for you while going through this chapter?

2

What Happens When We Don't Have Healthy Boundaries?

A life without healthy boundaries limits your ability to live your life on your own terms. What you want for yourself is clouded by what others say, think, and do. What *you* need is dimmed because of what others need. When you don't own and manage your life, others will do it for you.

People with unhealthy boundaries typically experience:

Burnout: Emotional, mental, and/or physical exhaustion

Resentment: Deep-rooted indignation about being mistreated

Frustration: Feeling annoyed when asked to do something

Anger: Hostility or annoyance, which might be expressed inwardly or outwardly

Superhero syndrome: Unreasonable belief that they can do everything, often without support from others

Anxiety: Setting unrealistic expectations, people-pleasing, and being unable to be assertive or say no

Depression: Hopelessness that life can change or that relationships can improve

Additionally, as a result of unhealthy boundaries, you might:

- Loan money to people when you don't have it to give
- Offer advice when it isn't requested
- Do things that you don't like
- Be codependent
- Complain about how others mistreat you
- Not have any time for yourself
- Give people several chances to hurt you
- Tell people more than you're comfortable sharing
- Feel resentful because you are overwhelmed
- Allow others to say things to you without speaking up for yourself
- Be frustrated by others whenever they request your support

You may need boundaries with:

- Your parents
- Your kids
- Your partner
- Your time
- Associates
- In-laws
- Family
- Friends
- Neighbors
- Exes
- Strangers

- Work
- Social media
- Yourself

Sometimes, healthy boundaries are about living your life according to your plans for your life. It's okay to listen to someone else's opinions, but stay mindful of who is offering their take on what's best for you. When people tell you what you "should" do, remember staying on track with your goals is adhering to your boundaries.

How you feel is a good indicator of whether you need to change your boundaries. For example, someone might say, "When I help my mother sort through her finances, I feel annoyed because I want her to know how to do it on her own. It would be helpful to teach her some of the strategies I'm using instead of doing it myself." Sometimes, we help people because we believe they can't do certain things on their own. In these instances, consider ways to empower them to be more self-sufficient or make use of other resources. This is particularly important when you can't or don't want to help.

EXERCISE

Consider the feelings listed below, and use them to complete the scenarios.

Angry	Guilty	Appreciated
Jealous	Thoughtful	Overwhelmed
Sad	Anxious	Stupid
Frustrated	Confused	Miserable
Resentful	Important	Skeptical

When I help _____ with _____, I feel
_____. It would be helpful to _____
_____ .

When I help _____ with _____, I feel
_____. It would be helpful to _____
_____ .

When I help _____ with _____, I feel
_____. It would be helpful to _____
_____ .

When I help _____ with _____, I feel
_____. It would be helpful to _____
_____ .

I haven't expressed my needs to _____
_____ about
_____ .

I haven't expressed my needs to _____
_____ about
_____ .

I haven't expressed my needs to _____
_____ about
_____ .

Seven Benefits of Setting Healthy Boundaries

1. You'll reduce any feelings of guilt.
2. You'll rid yourself of some unhealthy relationships.
3. Your healthy relationships will improve.
4. You'll discover your strength.
5. You'll create relationships that make you feel happy.

6. You'll learn to respect other people's boundaries.

7. You'll improve your ability to be assertive in multiple areas.

The "I Deserve Boundaries" Mindset

Repeat After Me: "I deserve healthy boundaries in my relationships with others and with myself. Boundaries are not mean and can be placed gently. Even when people don't like my boundaries, it doesn't mean I've done anything wrong by setting them."

Get it out of your head that you're a terrible person for setting boundaries, and remove the thought "boundaries are mean" from your mind and your mouth.

Boundaries make you a healthier friend.

Boundaries make you a healthier partner.

Boundaries make you a healthier parent.

Boundaries make you a healthier sister/brother.

Boundaries make you a healthier daughter/son.

Boundaries make you a healthier coworker.

Boundaries make you a healthier niece/nephew.

Boundaries make you a healthier family member.

Boundaries make you a healthier neighbor.

Boundaries make you a healthier human.

EXERCISE

Many people believe that saying no is the only way to set boundaries, but it's just a small part of the process. Before we move on to other parts of boundaries, let's practice a few ways to say no. For example, "Boundaries are a healthy way for me to heal."

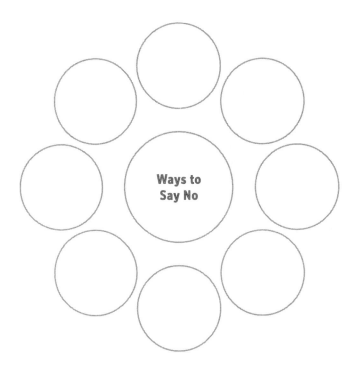

Ways to
Say No

Now, let's consider times when you might say yes. For each of the items mentioned, circle "yes," "maybe," or "no":

Helping a friend move	Yes	Maybe	No
Working on vacation	Yes	Maybe	No
Answering your phone when it's not a good time	Yes	Maybe	No
Pet-sitting for a friend	Yes	Maybe	No
Loaning a family member money	Yes	Maybe	No
Allowing family to visit you for the holidays	Yes	Maybe	No
_____	Yes	Maybe	No

	Yes	Maybe	No
_____	Yes	Maybe	No
_____	Yes	Maybe	No
_____	Yes	Maybe	No

For the ones you marked "maybe," what stopped you from clearly declaring "yes" or "no"? What are the exceptions? When you responded with "no," do you consistently say it in those areas?

_____

_____

_____

_____

_____

_____

_____

_____

_____

_____

EXERCISE

Part 1

Make a list of things you would like to start saying no to:

_____

_____

_____

_____

_____

_____

_____

_____

_____

_____

Part 2

I find it hard to say no to _____ because _____ .

I find it hard to say no to _____ because _____ .

I find it hard to say no to _____ because _____ .

I find it hard to say no to _____ because _____ .

I find it hard to say no to _____ because _____ .

I find it hard to say no to _____ because _____ .

I find it hard to say no to _____ because _____ .

I find it hard to say no to _____ because _____ .

Pause: At any point while going through this chapter, take a moment to close your eyes and envision a peaceful scene. For me, it's standing in front of the ocean on a warm summer day.

Common Reasons People Find It Hard to Say No

People-pleasing: "I want to be liked," or "I don't want anyone to be upset with me."

Fear: "If I say no, they will stop talking to me."

Unreasonable expectations: "I know I'm busy, but adding one more thing won't be too much trouble."

Common Negative-Thought Distortions That Make It Hard to Set Limits

Catastrophizing: Expecting the worst-case scenario. "If I set a boundary with my partner, they will leave me."

Personalizing: Taking things to heart or making things about you when they aren't. "It was my fault that they had too much to drink."

Overgeneralizing: Based on a single incident, developing a belief that things happen the same way all the time. "My friends can't help me because they have their own problems and aren't available."

Black-or-white thinking: Seeing things as one extreme or the other with no gray area. "People never care about what others want."

Jumping to conclusions: Expecting a negative outcome without trying. "They will never listen to me."

EXERCISE

Looking at the cognitive distortions above, which one or two have you used most often?

_____

_____

_____

_____

Instead of focusing on the worst-case scenario, what is a positive possible outcome?

_____

_____

_____

What affirmation (positive statement) can you use to increase your confidence in setting boundaries? Example: "I am worthy of healthy boundaries."

_____

_____

_____

_____

Unhealthy Alternatives to Setting Boundaries

Move Away

"I moved across town so that they would stop asking me to do things."

Gossip/Complain

"My coworker needs to budget better. It never fails. Three days before payday, I end up buying them lunch."

Avoid

"I don't visit my grandmother because she always says something about my weight."

Cut Off

"I stopped talking to my friend because she could never understand why she needs to be more respectful of my time."

JOURNAL PROMPT

What have you done to avoid setting boundaries with people or with yourself?

_____

_____

_____

_____

_____

_____

CHECKLIST

What has stopped you from setting boundaries? Put a check mark next to each behavior that has held you back:

- ❏ People-pleasing
- ❏ Self-sabotage
- ❏ Second-guessing yourself
- ❏ Fear
- ❏ Anxiety
- ❏ Guilt

How to Say No and Mean It

Consistency is the key to getting people to respect your boundaries. When placing a limit with others, say no, not maybe. Don't say, "Let me think about it" or "I will see what I can do." Using pacifying statements only leads people to believe that there's hope. You can be direct and still be a kind person.

Communicating your boundaries kindly sounds like this:
- "I care about you deeply. I can't help you with your issue."
- "I'm not able to support you financially, but I'm willing to support you in another way."
- "We need to reassess how we communicate, because it doesn't seem to be working for either of us."
- "Thank you for your request. I'm not available."
- "I know you love me and want the best for me. I would like it if you supported me by listening instead of offering feedback."
- "That sounds very challenging. I would love to help, but it seems like an issue that should be handled with a professional."

Nine Potential Reasons You Can't Sufficiently Set a Boundary
1. You fear being mean.
2. You fear being rude.
3. You're a people-pleaser.
4. You're anxious about future interactions after a boundary has been set.
5. You feel powerless and not sure that boundaries will help.
6. You get your value from helping others.
7. You project onto others your feelings about being told no.
8. You have no clue where to start.
9. You believe that you can't have boundaries in certain types of relationships.

Gather Yourself

What came up for you while going through this chapter?

3

Learning to Set Boundaries

Many of us are born aware of our needs. You knew when you were hungry or wet, or when you wanted to be comforted. Early on, you had no issues saying no and asking for what you needed. Somewhere along the way, we learn to quiet our desires for the comfort of others. This silencing creates adults who find it challenging to advocate for themselves. Someone may have told you, "It's not nice to do that," or ignored your needs.

In my book *Set Boundaries, Find Peace*, I wanted to help people get back to the root of who they were/are as boundaried individuals. You've been talked out of being assertive because it didn't please others. Reclaiming your voice is the key to setting boundaries.

JOURNAL PROMPT

What were some of the boundaries in your home?

Example: We were allowed to eat in the dining room only on holidays.

_____

_____

What boundaries do you think would've been helpful?

_____

_____

_____

_____

Did you feel safe setting boundaries in your family?

_____

_____

_____

_____

Be Clear and Make It Plain

Sometimes when people talk extensively about problems, boundaries become confusing. Nowhere in their lengthy description do they state a need or make a request. Therefore, when placing boundaries, it's important to get right down to what you want, need, and expect. Using more words doesn't make your boundary more valid, and providing lengthy explanations can give others ammunition to challenge your boundaries.

Three-Step Process

1. Keep it short. This is especially important if you're new to voicing your expectations. When you're a newbie, people can talk you out of your boundaries because of your lack of confidence. So keep your statements down to one or two sentences.

2. Be clear. Do your best to be as straightforward as possible. Mind your tone—don't yell or whisper. People will miss the boundary if you use complicated words or jargon. Take a deep, deep breath, and focus on being precise.

3. Directly state your need or request, or say no. Don't just mention what you don't like; ask for what you need or want. Identify your expectations, or decline the offer.

Use a starter:

Short version (beginners): I want/need/expect _____

_____.

Long version (more experienced):

I want _____ because _____

_____.

I need _____ because _____

_____.

I expect _____ because _____

_____.

Note: When using the long version, consider how you'll respond if they challenge your boundary.

Dealing with the discomfort that happens as a result of setting boundaries is the hardest part. Discomfort is the number one reason we bypass setting them. But it's common afterward to feel guilty, afraid, sad, remorseful, or awkward.

Examples:

A friend asks you to help them move, but you don't want to. You say, "I'm not able to help you move."

You're tired of hearing your friend complain about their partner. You say, "I want to be here for you, but I'm not able to help you. Have you considered a couples therapist?"

Try a few on your own:

A coworker is gossiping to you about another coworker, and you don't want to be involved.

_____

_____

You need help with planning your birthday party and want your sister to help.

_____

_____

_____

Pause: When you're feeling emotionally unable to move through the book, step outside for some fresh air.

Two Parts to Setting a Boundary: Verbal Communication and Action

It has always been assumed that boundaries are what we say to people, but boundaries are also what you do.

Examples of verbal boundaries:

"I'm not able to commit to another project at this time."

"I don't feel comfortable sharing something that isn't my business to share."

Examples of actions:

Not committing to more when you don't have the time to commit.

Not sharing anything when you feel uncomfortable doing so.

CHECKLIST

Have you ever experienced any of the following when you've set a boundary with someone?

- ❑ **Pushback:** They ignore that you mentioned a boundary and continue to do what they want.
- ❑ **Testing limits:** They try to sneak, manipulate, or get one past you. They attempt to do what they want but in a way you might not notice.
- ❑ **Rationalizing and questioning:** They challenge the reason for your boundary and its validity.
- ❑ **Defensiveness:** They challenge what you said or your character, or they make excuses about how their behavior is okay.

JOURNAL PROMPT

Write about how you felt when you experienced any reactions from the checklist on the previous page.

_____

_____

_____

_____

Gather Yourself

What came up for you while going through this chapter?

_____

_____

_____

_____

_____

_____

_____

_____

4

Managing the Discomfort
of Setting Boundaries

How You Respond to Your Boundaries

In 2020, Meghan Markle and Prince Harry announced they were leaving the royal family to create a different life for themselves. One year later, they were interviewed by Oprah Winfrey. In the interview, they discussed the chain of events leading to their separation from the royal family. After watching the interview, I posted this on Instagram:

> Let's allow Meghan Markle and Prince Harry to be shining examples of honoring our boundaries. Deciding to invent a life of your own may be different from what your family planned for you. Choosing to exist differently can change your relationships. When you execute your boundaries, some people will not be pleased. However, making decisions for yourself is brave and healthy. People cannot determine what's best for you. It's okay if what worked for others doesn't work for you.

You can be kind and set boundaries. Don't let trying to be nice stop you from doing the hard work of setting limits with others.

One of the most significant issues people have with boundaries is the discomfort associated with the process before, while, and after executing them. In this chapter, we will talk about managing your feelings.

It's Okay and Normal to Feel

They don't tell you in grad school that a considerable chunk of your time as a therapist will be spent telling clients, "It's okay to feel," and "What you're feeling is normal." I do this so often that after a while, my clients share how they feel and say, "I know what you're going to say: 'It's normal.'" Feelings are not bad, but some are uncomfortable.

We love to feel happy, excited, and overjoyed. But the moment we feel jealous, guilty, or frustrated, we want to stop the ability to feel. The neuroscientist Dr. Jill Taylor found that the typical emotion lasts about ninety seconds. According to Bryn Farnsworth, Ph.D., while emotions are associated with bodily reactions that are activated through neurotransmitters and hormones released by the brain, feelings are the conscious experience of emotional reactions.

With negative feelings, we tend to hang on for a very long time. Sometimes, we can be upset for an entire day or even a few days. But what we forget is that while upset, we likely experience other feelings simultaneously. We can feel more than one thing at the same time, but when we focus on the negative feeling, it seems as though it's all we're feeling.

This is *not* setting a boundary; it's controlling someone:
- Pushing someone to think and be like you
- Managing areas of someone's life that have no impact on you (i.e., not minding your own business)
- Determining what another person can or can't do with their life
- Demanding that people change for you
- Manipulating people into changing their behavior

- Creating rules for how others "should" do things in their life
- Telling people what's best for them

EXERCISE

To help illustrate the ability to have more than one feeling at a time, I will present a scenario, and I want you to describe at least two feelings about it. Then you will create your own scenarios.

As you're completing this exercise, please keep in mind that feelings are one word, such as "angry," "sad," or "confused." If you describe something in more detail, such as "I want to tell them to stop," chances are you're representing a thought or behavioral response. For this exercise, list only your feelings.

1. A friend asks you to join her for a movie night. Since you haven't seen her in a while, you agree. Just before leaving your house, your friend texts to cancel your plans.

   Name two initial feelings that come to mind when your friend cancels.

   _____

2. Create your own scenario, and name two or more feelings.

   _____

   _____

   _____

3. Create your own scenario, and name two or more feelings.

   _____

   _____

Guilt-Free Boundaries

"How do I set boundaries without feeling guilty?" My immediate thought is, "You can't." I know, I know—I'm a therapist; there must be something I can do to make boundaries guilt-free. I wish with all my therapist power that I could remove the guilt associated with setting boundaries, but I can't.

There are reasons we feel guilty:

1. We've done something wrong.
2. We think we're doing something wrong.

Because so many of us are programmed to believe that setting boundaries is mean or selfish, we feel guilty for placing expectations on our relationships with others. But we are entitled to healthy boundaries in our relationships.

Guilt is sometimes used as a control tactic in relationships to keep us compliant or make us feel bad for having needs. Other uncomfortable feelings include shame, jealousy, frustration, and anger.

Important Reminder: Sometimes when people don't want to adhere to your boundaries, they will make you seem irrational for having them. Instead of questioning yourself, accept that some people will make you feel like a difficult person for wanting healthy things for yourself no matter how logical your limits and expectations are. Your work is to determine how you wish to handle relationships with people who make healthy boundaries seem absurd.

EXERCISE

Feelings are an emotional state of being. It's essential to know how to connect your life experiences to your feelings, so in this exercise, I want you to practice naming uncomfortable feelings.

When was the last time you felt lonely?

What's the last situation that led to your feeling hurt?

What feeling do you feel most often?

What feeling is the most difficult for you to feel?

_____

_____

_____

What feeling do you talk about most often?

_____

_____

_____

Overwhelmed: doing more than you feel capable of doing, without enough perceived help

    Describe a time when you felt overwhelmed.

_____

_____

_____

Frustrated: distress and annoyance, mainly because of an inability to change or achieve something

    Describe a time when you felt frustrated.

_____

_____

_____

Embarrassed: shame or uncomfortable self-consciousness

   Describe a time when you felt embarrassed.

_____

_____

_____

_____

Jealous: feeling envy toward someone or their achievements and advantages

   Describe a time when you felt jealous.

_____

_____

_____

_____

Anxious: worried, uneasy, or nervous, typically about an imminent event or something with an uncertain outcome.

   Describe a time when you felt anxious.

_____

_____

_____

_____

Living with Feelings, Instead of Trying to Get Rid of Them

Sometimes, the only thing we can do about our feelings is allow them to flow, and sometimes, the only thing we can do is manage them. Your job is to figure out what you need.

When you're feeling uncomfortable, consider what you can do to manage the discomfort. For example, call a friend to help you.

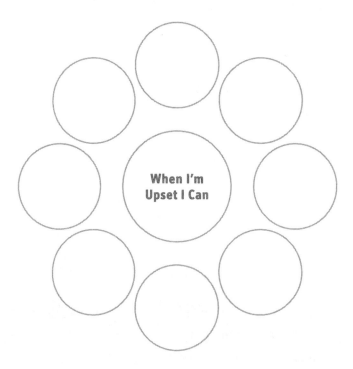

When I'm
Upset I Can

Uncomfortable Feelings May Arise from Setting Boundaries

Depending on your relationship with the other person, your connection to the situation, and how long you've gone without setting a boundary, you may experience discomfort (guilt, sadness, betrayal, or remorse).

Guilt

When you feel bad about making healthy choices for yourself, guilt may be a part of the process. The more comfortable you start to feel with setting boundaries, the less guilt you'll experience. Keep practicing as a way to reduce your guilt.

Repeat After Me: "Guilt is a symptom of believing that I did something wrong. It's possible to feel guilty even when I am doing something right. If I have not done anything to harm another person, my guilt is not appropriate or helpful. I am not responsible for everything that someone else feels. I am responsible for honoring my needs, and sometimes that means that others will not be able to get their way."

Sadness

Because you don't want to hurt anyone's feelings, you may feel sad about executing a boundary. Even when you don't know how someone else feels, you may feel sad at the thought of making someone else feel sad. It's healthy to be empathetic, and your feelings are a sign that you care about others.

Betrayal

Setting limits with others does not mean that you don't love them. Consider boundaries as a way to keep your relationships healthy while honoring yourself and the other person. You aren't doing anything to harm them or the relationship. Your intention is to keep the relationship strong.

Remorse

Don't betray yourself to please others by saying something like, "Did I say that? Oh my gosh, that came out wrong." It's natural to feel like you didn't do the right thing after you set a boundary. But it isn't wrong or bad to set them. Reframe the way you think about boundaries, and that mental shift will help you minimize discomfort.

JOURNAL PROMPT

How would implementing or reshaping your boundaries positively change your relationships with the significant people in your life?

_____

_____

_____

_____

_____

_____

_____

How Others Respond to Your Boundaries
Emotional Maturity

Emotional maturity impacts a person's ability to receive, understand, and implement boundaries. People have a right to a reaction, but it's inappropriate when their reaction causes harm to another person. When you express an expectation, some people will indeed not like it. Know that their reaction is a reflection of their emotional maturity and experience.

Chronological age is not an indicator of someone's maturity. Life experiences, knowledge, and comprehension are all factors that influence it. For example, suppose you've done the work of learning about yourself, and you're speaking to someone unfamiliar with the process of self-reflection. In that case, they may not understand your perspective. It's essential to remember that someone's experiences and understanding may impact how they perceive your boundaries.

Handling an Unhealthy Reaction to Your Boundaries

Step 1

Restate your boundary.

I need _____
_____ .

Step 2

Communicate a consequence if your boundary is not respected.

If you aren't able to do _____
_____ , I will _____
_____ .

Important Reminder: Do not set a limit that you can't maintain. The consequence of not respecting your boundary needs to be something you can follow through with. For example, "I need you to ask me a few days in advance to babysit. If you ask me the day you need me, it's possible I won't be available."

Step 3

Manage your discomfort by referring to the "When I'm Upset I Can . . ." diagram you created earlier in this chapter.

Important Reminder: Sometimes, the very people shaming you for making choices without their input, taking care of yourself, and standing firm in your boundaries are the same people who need to practice trusting themselves, taking care of themselves, and having healthy boundaries of their own. Because it's hard for them, they may try to make it hard for you. When you know the other person struggles to stand in their power, perhaps their pushing back is a sign that you're on the right track.

Gather Yourself

In this chapter, we talked about discomfort. Think about what or who contributes to your feelings of discomfort around setting boundaries. Write about them below:

_____

_____

_____

_____

_____

_____

_____

_____

_____

_____

5

Knowing Your Boundaries

It's hard to know when a boundary is being violated when you don't know you're entitled to set and maintain boundaries at all. In 2020, *Black Panther* actor Chadwick Boseman died. To fans and many people, it was shocking. Some began to question why Chadwick kept his diagnosis of cancer a secret. On my Instagram account, I wrote this:

> Let's allow Chadwick Boseman to be a shining example of honoring our boundaries. He shared his health issues with the people he chose and continued to live his dream. We can keep things to ourselves. We can be private. Privacy is not secret-keeping; it's sharing with trusted loved ones and sharing with others when we are ready. Privacy is a healthy boundary. You do not owe anyone more than you are comfortable sharing. People are not entitled to know your personal business.

> Privacy is a boundary, and you can share as much or as little as you want.

The Six Types of Boundaries

Physical

Personal space and physical touch are your physical boundaries. Your physical space is the perimeter around your body. We all have a certain level of awareness of our body and what feels comfortable to us, and everyone's needs in terms of physical space are different. People also have different views as to what types and amounts of physical touch are appropriate. These boundaries vary depending on the setting and situation, the relationship we have with the other person, and our comfort level. But we can tell people our preferences about personal space and physical touch.

Sexual

It's never okay to touch anyone's body without consent, and children can never consent to sexual acts. Touching, making sexual comments, or engaging in sexual acts without expressed consent violate sexual boundaries. It's never acceptable for children to be placed in any sexual situation—even a sexual conversation in their presence. Since children can't communicate sexual limits, adults must adhere to appropriate behavior with children.

Unlike other boundaries that need to be spoken to be understood, many sexual ones are unspoken because they are society's rules. These include rape, assault, and molestation. There are laws against forcible sexual acts. However, many things that are not illegal can violate someone's boundaries, such as talking about someone's body in a way that makes them uncomfortable. You can speak your boundaries about your body to guide people in communicating with you physically or verbally.

Intellectual

Intellectual boundaries refer to your thoughts and ideas. You're free to have an opinion about anything you want. And when you express your opinion, your words shouldn't be dismissed, belittled, or ridiculed.

However, staying mindful of what topics are appropriate versus inappropriate in a specific situation is another way of respecting intellectual boundaries. When a parent has an inappropriate conversation with a child, it's an intellectual boundary violation.

Remember This: Sometimes, the boundary is living your life according to your plans for yourself. It's okay to listen to others when what they say is valuable and helpful, but it's also good to stay mindful of who is offering their take about what's best for you. When people tell you what you "should" do, know that staying on track with your goals is adhering to your boundaries.

Emotional

When you share your feelings, it's reasonable to expect others to support you. For some of us, expressing emotions isn't easy. So when someone belittles your emotions or invalidates your feelings, they are violating your emotional boundaries. This can make you feel uncomfortable the next time you want to express what you feel.

With healthy emotional boundaries, you express your feelings and personal information to others gradually, not all at once. This also means you share only when it's appropriate, and you choose your confidants carefully.

Remember This: Sometimes, a boundary with yourself means sharing only what you want other people to know while keeping the rest to yourself. You have a right to privacy even when people request more information. Others don't have to understand your boundaries to honor them.

Material

Material boundaries have to do with your possessions. Your stuff is your stuff. If you decide to share your stuff, it's your choice. You also have the right to determine how others treat your possessions. If you loan a tool in good condition to a friend, it's appropriate to expect the tool to be returned in the same shape. When someone returns something in worse condition or doesn't return it at all, they've violated your material boundaries.

Time

Time boundaries consist of how you manage your time, how you allow others to use your time, how you deal with favor requests, and how you structure your free time. People with time boundary issues struggle with work-life balance, self-care, and prioritizing their needs. Giving up your time to others is one significant way that you might violate your time boundaries. If you don't have time for something that you want to do, you don't have healthy boundaries with time.

EXERCISE

Now that you're familiar with the six types of boundaries, let's practice. For each of the six types, write a boundary that you would like to set for yourself.

Physical

_____

_____

_____

_____

Sexual

Intellectual

Emotional

Material

Time

_____

_____

_____

For each of the six boundary types, describe a way that your boundary has
been violated.

Physical

_____

_____

_____

_____

_____

Sexual

_____

_____

_____

_____

Intellectual

Emotional

Material

_____

_____

_____

_____

_____

Time

_____

_____

_____

_____

_____

Pause: Take a moment to reflect on your words before moving on, and take a few moments to breathe if you need to.

Sometimes, it's easier to see when others violate our boundaries, and it's less obvious to see when we are overstepping others' boundaries.

Impeding on someone else's boundaries doesn't make you a bad person.

Most often, it happens because we're unaware of what makes a relationship healthy or unhealthy. Whether you have intentionally or unintentionally violated someone's boundaries, it's essential to be honest with yourself.

EXERCISE

"I have dishonored other people's boundaries in the following ways . . ."

Physical

_____

_____

_____

_____

Sexual

_____

_____

_____

_____

Intellectual

Emotional

Material

Time

_____

_____

_____

_____

_____

_____

JOURNAL PROMPT

After acknowledging how you've violated someone else's boundaries, write about how these revelations about yourself make you feel.

_____

_____

_____

_____

Micro Violations

Boundary micro violations are small violations that often occur in everyday encounters, as opposed to long-term relationships. We aren't usually as emotionally affected by them, and they don't spill over into the rest of our day, because we don't view the encounters as significant. Micro boundary violations can become more important over time, however, if they are repeated and persistent.

Examples of micro boundary violations:
1. You decline a lunch invitation from your coworker. Over the next two days, your usually chatty coworker doesn't speak to you.
2. You are standing in line at the store and trying to maintain a six-foot distance. Despite signage posted and your attempts to create space, the person behind you is standing too close.

Addressing micro violations eliminates the opportunity for things to evolve into macro violations. Also, addressing the micro offense may give you the courage to address the macro offenses.

Macro Violations

Boundary macro violations are significant violations that erode the fabric of our relationships with others. These are long-standing and persistent. Their frequency and intensity can even change the structure of a relationship.

Examples of macro boundary violations:
1. Whenever you discuss financial achievements with your brother, he asks to borrow money.
2. Your parents gossip about your siblings' relationships with their partners. It makes you feel uncomfortable to be involved in the conversation.

EXERCISE

Please list the boundary issues in each category that you've experienced in your relationships.

Micro Boundary Issues   Macro Boundary Issues

_____   _____

_____   _____

_____   _____

_____   _____

_____   _____

_____   _____

Gather Yourself

This chapter encouraged you to look at how your boundaries are violated and how you might violate other people's boundaries. After identifying how you've violated someone else's boundaries, practice being compassionate with yourself. Forgive yourself, and do better going forward.

_____

_____

_____

6

How to Speak Your Boundaries
(So People Can Hear You)

Three Steps to Setting a Boundary

Step 1

Be clear, and focus on the solution, not the problem.

Often when we think we're setting boundaries, we are mostly talking about the problem. The boundary is the solution. What would you like? What do you want to see next time? What would make you feel safe? Going over a problem without discussing the solution will lead people to repeat the behavior causing the issue. Sometimes, the person who is causing a problem may be unaware of alternative solutions, or simply doesn't know what your limit is.

You should be able to condense what you need into one or two sentences, maximum. For example, "I'm not able to take care of your plants while you're on vacation."

Not this: "I don't know why you asked me to care for your plants while you're on vacation. You know I have a black thumb. The last time you asked me to watch your plants, one died, and you complained about my ability to care for them. Why don't you ask someone who knows more about plants?"

Also not this: "You should ask your sister to water your plants instead."

Remember, the boundary is the solution. It's up to the other person to make new arrangements.

It's imperative to be clear and concise, particularly if you are new to setting boundaries. People can find your weaknesses if you aren't secure in what you're saying. As a result, they can easily talk you out of your boundary. As you become more confident in setting boundaries, you can add more to your explanation, but remain clear and concise. You don't have to explain your need for safety. It's okay if what you need looks different from what others need.

Step 2

State what you need and want, or say no.

Speak your truth in the following ways:

I want . . .

I need . . .

I expect . . .

Next time . . .

Step 3

Manage your discomfort.

It's normal to feel guilt, fear, sadness, remorse, awkwardness, indifference, or relief when setting boundaries. Guilt is often the most challenging part of the process, but it's to be expected, especially if you're new to it. Guilt shows that you are emotionally aware and are concerned about potentially hurting others. But don't let your guilt stop you from doing what you need for your well-being.

Also, after setting a boundary, it's normal to feel relieved. The hard part is over. You did it! And even when people aren't happy with your boundaries, it feels good to get the fundamental hard part out of the way.

EXERCISE

Name someone in your family who has said things that led you to feel guilty for honoring yourself. What was the boundary?

_____

_____

_____

_____

_____

_____

Name a friend who has said things that led you to feel guilty for honoring yourself. What was the boundary?

_____

_____

_____

_____

_____

_____

Name a partner (past or present) who has said things that led you to feel guilty for honoring yourself. What was the boundary?

_____

_____

_____

_____

_____

A few ways to manage discomfort:

- Feel it (just sit with it, without pushing it away or doing anything)
- Journal
- Move your body
- Call a friend
- Cry
- Watch something funny
- Hug someone
- Take a nap
- Tap into a creative outlet

- _____

- _____

What to Say and How to Say It

The hardest part is finding the right words. But there aren't any absolutely "right" words. When helping my clients figure out how to speak their needs to others, I often find myself saying, "You already have the words." But it makes sense that we want to practice what to say over and over because we don't want to offend or hurt someone. Just know that while there aren't perfect "right" words, there *are* wrong words that you want to avoid. These include demeaning others or attacking someone's character. As long as you don't do that, your words will be *right*.

EXERCISE

Let's practice what to say. In this exercise, focus on what you're trying to convey and not on wanting to please the other person.

1. A friend asks you to dog-sit for two weeks while they visit family. You don't want to take on the task, because in the past the dog whined and kept you up at night.

    What do you say to your friend?

2. You have plans for your birthday, and your partner keeps insisting that you should do something other than what you have planned. You want to stick to your plans.

What do you say to your partner?

_____

_____

_____

_____

_____

3. Your mother stays in touch with your ex after the terrible breakup between the two of you. She says that despite what you experienced with your ex, their relationship remains intact. Your mother brings up their interactions often, and it makes you uncomfortable.

What do you say to your mother?

_____

_____

_____

_____

_____

4. When you and your best friend became roommates, you assumed they would pitch in to clean the house. Your feelings about how your friend maintains the house are starting to impact your desire to engage with them.

   What do you say to your friend?

   _____

   _____

   _____

   _____

   _____

   _____

Let's practice saying:
- "I would like you to listen instead of offering solutions."
- "I feel more than one way, and I don't have to pick one way to feel."
- "I feel unsafe in this interaction."
- "Please respect my decision."
- "I don't feel comfortable sharing with you because you tend to tell me what's best for me instead of listening."
- "I need a few moments to myself."
- "I need to vent. Do you have a moment to listen?"
- "I'm not looking for advice. I just want to vent."
- "This isn't the best time for me to talk. I will call you back when I can give you my full attention."
- "I know you meant well, but what you said wasn't helpful."

- "How would you like me to support you?"
- "I need your help with _____."

Five Ways to Communicate a Boundary

Passive: denying or ignoring your needs to allow others to be comfortable

Aggressive: having rigid and inflexible standards of how to engage with others; applying strict rules to all people; sharing boundaries in an abrasive manner or doing so to offend

Passive-aggressive: having boundaries but not making them clear to others; assuming that people know your boundaries and then getting frustrated when your boundaries are violated

Manipulative: issuing ultimatums to be punitive; threatening to do things you won't follow through on

Assertive: having clear and concise expectations

EXERCISE

In the scenarios below, identify if the boundary is expressed in a way that feels passive, aggressive, passive-aggressive, manipulative, or assertive.

1. Your boss emails you while you're on vacation.

   Your response: When you return to work, you give your boss the cold shoulder for the day because they should've known better than to bother you while on vacation.

   What type of response did you have? _____

2. Your father calls you by your family nickname in front of friends and in public places. You would prefer him to call you by your given name.

Your response: You don't mention it to your dad because it's what he has always done.

What type of response did you have? _____

3. You're invited to a Zoom birthday celebration at the same time as another online event you prepaid for.

Your response: "Thank you for the invitation, but I won't be able to attend."

What type of response did you have? _____

4. Your brother asks you to store a few things in your garage while he moves. He promises to have everything out within a month. It's been one year, and his things are still in your garage.

Your response: Every month, you call him to tell him to get his things or you will throw them out.

What type of response did you have? _____

5. Your food delivery order was not prepared correctly.

Your response: You call the restaurant, yelling and cussing at the manager because you're pissed off.

What type of response did you have? _____

Key: 1. Passive-aggressive; 2. Passive; 3. Assertive; 4. Manipulative; 5. Aggressive

Pause: Take a moment to listen to the sounds in your environment. What are they? How do they make you feel?

Because setting a boundary is challenging, let's practice a little bit more.

EXERCISE

Look at the list of five ways to communicate a boundary, and write an example for each of the ways using the following scenario:

An acquaintance, a friend of a friend, asks you to plan their milestone birthday party.

Passive:

_____

_____

Aggressive:

_____

_____

Passive-aggressive:

_____

_____

Manipulative:

_____

_____

Assertive:

_____

_____

Your coworker asks you to pay when you grab lunch, saying they'll pay you back. They haven't paid you back from the last time you grabbed lunch.

Passive:

_____

_____

Aggressive:

_____

_____

Passive-aggressive:

_____

_____

Manipulative:

_____

_____

Assertive:

_____

_____

Your friend's partner makes inappropriate comments about your weight in front of your friend, who doesn't defend you.

Passive:

_____

_____

Aggressive:

_____

_____

Passive-aggressive:

_____

_____

Manipulative:

_____

_____

Assertive:

_____

_____

Provide an example of when someone has communicated a boundary with you in the following ways.

Passive:

_____

_____

Aggressive:

_____

_____

Passive-aggressive:

_____

_____

Manipulative:

_____

_____

Assertive:

_____

_____

Note: Pay close attention to how you implement your boundaries. It's expected that when you first start expressing limits, you may go at full throttle and be slightly aggressive. Learn as you go.

Assertiveness sounds like this:
- "My food wasn't prepared properly. I want a refund."
- "I'm not satisfied with my haircut. I would like you to fix it."
- "The next time you're going to be late, please let me know ahead of time."
- "I don't think it's funny to talk about my weight."
- "I don't want to talk about having kids."
- "I'm not seeking feedback."
- "I'm speaking."
- "I don't want to talk about my dating life."
- "I feel supported when you honor my wishes."

How to Handle People Who Don't Listen to Your Boundaries

No matter how assertive you are, there may be some people who challenge your boundaries. When this happens, it's important to remember that you are doing something healthy for yourself.

JOURNAL PROMPT

What are your thoughts and feelings about setting boundaries with difficult people?

List a few affirmations that might help you follow through with your boundaries.

Examples:

"Despite my feeling of guilt, I am acting in my best interest."

"I can push through even when there is pushback."

_____

_____

_____

_____

Reimagine Your Beliefs About Boundaries

As you practice what could go wrong, it's important to consider that things could and often do go better than expected. In this next exercise, I want you to consider something positive happening.

BOUNDARY	CHALLENGING THOUGHT	POSITIVE POSSIBILITY
"I want to stay at a hotel when I visit my family."	They will be hurt and disappointed because they are used to me staying with them.	My family will understand my desire for space, and we'll be able to have a nice visit that feels less tense for me.

Repeat After Me: "I am not responsible for how people respond to my boundaries. I am responsible for setting and honoring my boundaries. If my relationships end because I set boundaries, it's a sign that the foundation was cracked. In healthy relationships, I can set boundaries without fear of retaliation, cutoffs, or manipulation."

Six Steps to Setting Boundaries with Challenging People
1. Assertively restate the boundary as needed.
2. Correct the violation in real time. Don't let the opportunity pass and then mention it later. Say it in the moment.
3. Be consistent with implementing your boundaries.
4. Accept that they, although difficult, are entitled to their response even if it's different from the one you'd like.
5. Choose not to take it personally. They want to do what they want to do. You're asking them to do something uncomfortable that's likely difficult for them.
6. Manage your discomfort.

EXERCISE

Decide how you want to respond to the people who are especially challenging to set boundaries with by brainstorming responses.

When _____ violates my boundary regarding _____
_____, I will _____.
_____.

When _____ violates my boundary regarding _____
_____, I will _____
_____.

When _____ violates my boundary regarding _____
_____, I will _____
_____.

When _____ violates my boundary regarding _____
_____, I will _____
_____.

Gather Yourself

Remember, practice is an essential part of getting better at setting and maintaining boundaries. The more you move through the workbook and familiarize yourself with different strategies, the more confident you'll feel about saying complicated things.

What came up for you while going through this chapter?

_____

_____

_____

_____

_____

_____

_____

7

Getting Better at Communicating Your Boundaries

In some relationships, we function with unhealthy behaviors for years. With unhealthy boundaries well established, many of us are unsure how to shift once we become aware of the need for change.

You Don't Have to Remain the Same When You Know Better

A hallmark of wisdom is knowing when it's time to abandon some of your most treasured tools—and some of the most cherished parts of your identity.

—ADAM GRANT

One of my favorite phrases is "until today," which is also the title of a book by Iyanla Vanzant. In my life, I interpret it as meaning that even though I may have accepted something or engaged in certain habits for years, I can choose to stop now. There is no rule saying that we have to stay the same just because people expect us to never change.

Throughout life, we go through so many changes. From childhood to adulthood, we experience countless shifts in interests and needs and how we respond when they're not being met. It makes sense, because we are never finished evolving.

Important Reminder: Some of the people you have problematic relationships with will never change. When you accept people as they are, you can consciously decide if you want to continue in the relationship. If you aren't ready to leave a relationship, being aware of who others are will help you determine how you show up in the relationship. You have choices. You can be different, even if they won't change.

SELF-ASSESSMENT

Are you prepared to set new boundaries in your existing relationships? Where are you currently functioning?

Rate the statements below on a scale of 1 to 5 to describe where you are in your boundary journey. At the end, add up your total score.

1 = rarely
2 = occasionally
3 = frequently
4 = most of the time
5 = always

1. I believe that healthy boundaries are important for relationships.
   1 2 3 4 5
2. I believe that I am entitled to have healthy boundaries in my relationships.
   1 2 3 4 5
3. I believe that others are entitled to have healthy boundaries with me.
   1 2 3 4 5
4. I'm comfortable communicating my limits and expectations to others.
   1 2 3 4 5

5. Worrying how others might respond impacts my ability to set healthy boundaries.

   1 2 3 4 5

6. I feel comfortable restating my boundaries to others.

   1 2 3 4 5

7. I can choose to act in my best interests.

   1 2 3 4 5

8. People are aware of my needs.

   1 2 3 4 5

9. When my needs change, I communicate them.

   1 2 3 4 5

10. I feel comfortable asking for support.

   1 2 3 4 5

Scoring

41–50: You are healthy and secure in your practice and adhere to healthy boundaries. Refreshing or restating your boundaries isn't usually a challenge for you. Keep up the good therapeutic work.

31–40: You're doing a good job. Continue to improve on the skills you have.

21–30: The application of this work is challenging to maintain. Sometimes you do a good job, and other times you slack on the principles. Practice being more consistent and becoming more confident in your boundaries.

11–20: You struggle to understand and implement boundaries. Keep working through the exercises in this book, revisiting them as needed.

0–10: Focus on gaining more foundational skills, such as building boundaries, understanding the importance of having healthy expectations, and learning how to communicate your needs. Your journey has just begun.

Correcting Boundary Mishaps

Implementing Too Many New Things at Once

Learning new information can make us excited to share what we've learned and put it into practice. Often, we have so many new expectations that we attempt to share them all at once. But if you express too many of your needs at the same time, the other person will be unlikely to be receptive.

Stating the Problem Without Sharing the Solution

Instead of stating the boundary, perhaps you shared your issues. That's a step toward something, but it probably isn't clear enough to either express what you need or to actually say no.

Being Aggressive

Perhaps you yelled, screamed, cursed, or berated someone because you wanted to be heard. Aggressiveness makes a bigger problem than the problem you're trying to solve.

Being Inconsistent

The key to getting people to respect your boundaries is consistency. When you are inconsistent in upholding your limits and expectations, people will be inconsistent in honoring them.

EXERCISE

In this exercise, identify a few scenarios when you experienced a boundary mishap.

1. Mishap:

_____

_____

Outcome following the mishap:

Corrective action:

2. Mishap:

Outcome following the mishap:

Corrective action:

_____

_____

_____

3. Mishap:

_____

_____

_____

Outcome following the mishap:

_____

_____

_____

Corrective action:

_____

_____

_____

Shifting Gears

If you allow your boundaries to be violated because you're afraid or uncomfortable, you will continue suffering. When you're ready to implement new boundaries, do so slowly. Start slow and address one item at a time. It's often helpful to start with the issue that troubles you most. Prioritize the important boundaries first, and once you've been successful with one, move on to the next.

Let's take a look at some critical boundary areas. Think of something that has been allowed to occur for a long time, and decide what boundary you'd like to set to change the situation. Remember to start your statement with "*I want*," "*I need*," "*I expect*," or "*I will say no to* . . ."

Romantic relationships

Friendships

Work/School

Family relationships

_____

_____

_____

Social media

_____

_____

_____

Refresh Your Boundaries as Needed

We don't stay the same, and neither do our needs in relationships. As you change and become more self-aware, it makes sense that what you need or don't want will change. In 2020, the world experienced an unprecedented shift caused by COVID-19. Many people had to adjust their boundaries and expectations during that time. Home became the hub for work, school, exercise, and so much more. And if you shared space with others, accommodating everyone was an additional stressor. Restructuring boundaries in the pandemic is how many people were able to survive.

The Three Cs

Clear

Concise

Consistent

To ensure that you're setting effective boundaries, ask yourself these questions:

1. Was my boundary clear? Were they paying attention? Did I state what I needed, say no, or set a limit?
2. Was the boundary concise? Did I overexplain myself or use complicated language?
3. Did I follow through on the boundary? How am I upholding my boundary?

Pause: COVID-19 was shocking and impactful. Take a few moments to be mindful before moving on to the next exercise, which addresses the impact of the pandemic on our relationships and ourselves.

EXERCISE: COVID-19 CHANGED THE WAY WE VIEWED THE WORLD

How did the pandemic impact you most?

_____

_____

_____

_____

_____

_____

Did the pandemic change your relationship with others? If so, how?

_____

_____

_____

_____

_____

What were some new limits you set with yourself or others during this time?

_____

_____

_____

_____

What difficult conversations did you have with others?

_____

_____

_____

_____

_____

_____

_____

Are there lasting changes you want to implement going forward?

_____

_____

_____

_____

_____

You Can Clean Up Your Mess

Perhaps you missed the opportunity to speak up in a specific circumstance, or you said too much. There's still time to be more efficient. I encourage you to use what we have talked about thus far, go back loaded with new information, and set new boundaries. You may not always get it right, but thank goodness there's a next time. Clean up the mess you may have made, and apologize if necessary. You didn't know what you didn't know. Practice what you've learned going forward, and don't be afraid to go back and fix things.

Gather Yourself

Repeat the following affirmation:

"I may not always get it right, because being human doesn't require being perfect."

What came up for you while going through this chapter?

_____

_____

_____

_____

_____

_____

_____

_____

_____

_____

_____

8

How Your Childhood Impacts
Your Adult Boundaries

Childhood and adult trauma impact the way we perceive and engage in the world around us. Types of trauma can range from sexual abuse to witnessing a car accident. Indications of trauma are evident in how people respond. For example, the adult child of an alcoholic may fear driving because they frequently rode in the car with a drunk parent behind the wheel.

SELF-ASSESSMENT
What type of trauma have you experienced? Please check each box that applies.

- ❏ Emotional abuse
- ❏ Neglect (physical or emotional)
- ❏ Bullying
- ❏ Sexual abuse, sexual assault, or rape
- ❏ Having an absent parent
- ❏ Physical abuse or physical violence
- ❏ Death of a loved one
- ❏ Pregnancy loss
- ❏ Verbal abuse

- ❏ Car accident
- ❏ Infertility
- ❏ Raised by caregivers who abused substances
- ❏ Death of a friend
- ❏ Near-death experience
- ❏ Difficult breakup
- ❏ Chronic health issues
- ❏ Witnessed a violent or an abusive event

Childhood Trauma

Adults live with the scars of childhood trauma, and in many cases, it affects how we engage in relationships. It may also affect our attachments with the people and things in our lives.

Adults carry the following from childhood:

- Engaging in unhealthy relationships
- Self-sabotage
- Low self-esteem
- Addiction
- Codependency
- Unhealthy boundaries
- Perfectionism
- Emotional unavailability
- Guilt when caring for self
- Guilt for healing

Saying no and setting expectations is especially demanding for us when it wasn't taught or honored in childhood.

LET'S EXPLORE YOUR STORY

Do you remember your early boundaries?

_____

_____

_____

_____

_____

Who was the first person to honor one of your boundaries?

_____

_____

_____

_____

_____

What was the boundary?

_____

_____

Who was the first person to dishonor your boundary?

What was the boundary?

Pause: Before moving on to the next exercise, take a break from the work if you need to, and return to it when you feel centered. If you feel comfortable moving forward, take a few moments to breathe before continuing.

EXERCISE

When I was a child, this would have been a helpful boundary:

_____

_____

_____

_____

_____

I felt heard and seen by the following people:

_____

_____

_____

_____

_____

I wanted to be seen by these people:

_____

_____

_____

_____

_____

I recall my caregivers having the following rules for me:

_____

_____

_____

_____

_____

I remember having the following boundaries for myself:

_____

_____

_____

If I said no in my house, the following happened:

I wish my caregivers would've taught me this:

I think adults should honor the following boundaries with children:

_____

_____

_____

_____

_____

_____

_____

Affirmation

I will no longer use the excuse "my parents never taught me" as a reason to not do better. I can teach myself by reading, by being open to learning, by being curious, and by connecting to healthy people. I can find support through mentors, role models, elders, or mental health professionals. I can learn things that I was never taught, including how to be in healthy relationships, how to feel, how to care for myself, how to be assertive, and how to deal with problems in a healthy way.

Understanding What You Need from Others

When you share your experience from a traumatic event, compassionate support can facilitate your healing. Let's practice ways of asking for what you need.

Brainstorm a few ways to ask for support, and try to be specific about what works for you. For example, "When I cry, please rub my back, and tell me everything will be okay."

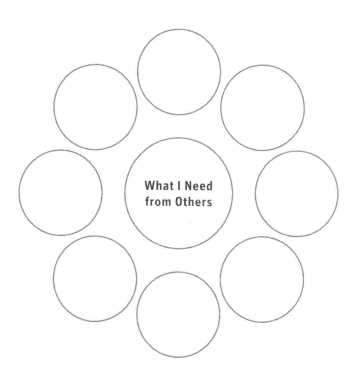

What I Need from Others

Guilt

A normal but not always helpful response to trauma is guilt—the kind of guilt that may cause you to feel bad about yourself and sometimes do unhealthy things.

Real guilt: You did something wrong.

False guilt: You believe you did something wrong, but you didn't.

To wash your hands of guilt that isn't yours to carry, complete the following statements:

When _____ happened, it was not my fault.

When _____ happened, it was not my fault.

When _____ happened, it was not my fault.

When _____ happened, it was not my fault.

Remember This: You can feel guilty when you aren't doing anything wrong. Guilt may be a part of your conditioning. You can unlearn the belief that everything is your fault or that you have done something harmful to others. The way to feel less guilty is to practice placing boundaries within yourself and with others. Do the work until it feels normal and habitual for you. The guilt will subside as you retrain your brain not to blame yourself for what others feel or experience.

You Can Say No

A two-year-old's favorite word is "no," and they say it with conviction because they feel entitled not to like, want, or be something that doesn't feel right. You can tap into your inner two-year-old and boldly reclaim your ability to say no with the belief that you are entitled to it.

When was the last time someone told you no?

What have you recently said no to?

How did it make you feel at the time?

How do you feel about it now?

_____

_____

_____

_____

Why did you say no?

_____

_____

_____

_____

Ways to say no now:

_____

_____

_____

_____

EXERCISE: TRAUMA AND BOUNDARIES

When I was younger, I responded to my trauma in the following ways:

_____

_____

_____

_____

_____

_____

As an adult, I respond to my trauma in the following ways:

_____

_____

_____

_____

_____

_____

Gather Yourself

Using the blank bullet points below, create your own affirming statements.

- I can teach myself what I wish my parents would've taught me.
- I forgive myself for blaming myself when things weren't my fault.
- I recognize that some people won't apologize or recognize what they did as "wrong."
- I can be for myself what I need from others.
- I can't forget what happened, but I can learn to cope with what happened.
- I am not alone.
- I can create a healthy life.
- I don't have to repeat the cycle.

- _____

_____

- _____

_____

- _____

_____

- _____

_____

- _____

_____

- _____

_____

9

Holding Your Boundaries Is a Form of Self-Care

Self-care is a restorative mental, spiritual, emotional, and physical practice that rejuvenates, relaxes, and enhances your life. It's personal—therefore, how you practice self-care may look different from the way someone else practices it.

Although self-care is used in response to feeling overwhelmed or depleted, it's also a preventative practice.

What things do you do on a daily basis to take care of yourself?

_____

_____

_____

_____

_____

_____

What are some of your thoughts and beliefs about taking care of yourself?

_____

_____

_____

_____

_____

What gets in the way of you taking better care of yourself?

_____

_____

_____

_____

_____

What boundaries do you need to set for yourself and others to have more time for self-care?

_____

_____

_____

_____

_____

_____

Leaning into Yourself

The most reported problem with practicing self-care is the inability to find time for it. In this exercise, consider the time you spend doing the following activities in one day and over one week.

ACTIVITY	TIME PER DAY	TIME PER WEEK
Watching TV		
Using social media		
Doing household work		
Going to work/school		
Playing video games		
Sleeping		
Caring for others		
Dating/spending time with a partner		
Engaging in a hobby		
Spending time with others		
Spending time alone		
Doing things you enjoy		
Doing things you don't enjoy		

Others are engaged in self-nurturing practices all around you.

I see my friends caring for themselves in the following ways:

_____

_____

_____

_____

I see my partner practicing self-care in the following ways:

_____

_____

_____

_____

I saw my parents/caregivers caring for themselves in the following ways:

_____

_____

_____

_____

When people don't care for themselves, I've noticed the following consequences:

_____

_____

_____

_____

_____

_____

In what ways can you better care for yourself in the following areas?

Physical	Spiritual
Mental	Emotional

Personal Boundaries

It's healthy to have limits with yourself. Some of us don't like being told what to do by others, so we're challenged by setting rules for ourselves. You can't do whatever you want because doing so could damage your health, relationships, and goals.

PERSONAL BOUNDARY ASSESSMENT

Let's go deeper with the following exercise. For each statement, identify if you have healthy boundaries in the specified area.

	HEALTHY	UNHEALTHY
Finances		
Self-care		
Physical care		
Mental health		
Spiritual care		
Relationships		

Self-Boundaries Are Self-Discipline

An essential part of setting boundaries involves honoring the limits you've set with others and yourself. Practicing boundaries is an act of shifting your habits. The next time you become upset when someone dishonors your boundary, consider how challenging it is to discipline yourself to always uphold your boundaries.

My biggest challenge with honoring limitations that I set for myself is:

_____

_____

_____

_____

_____

I violate the boundaries I set for myself in the following ways:

When I dishonor my boundaries, I can tell myself:

Forcing People to Honor Your Needs Isn't Possible

Healthy boundaries are about are you, not other people. You can choose how you want to show up, but you cannot make (force or demand that) others be anything except who they want to be. Essentially, you are making requests of others that they have the choice to honor or not.

Controlling others, particularly when their behaviors have nothing to do with you, is not healthy. Just as you have expectations, other people can have expectations for themselves. Just as you are entitled to live your life, other people are entitled to live theirs.

Sometimes, what you want collides with what the other person wants. In these cases, you have choices: Which need is healthiest? Can you compromise? And if you can't resolve it on your own, consider consulting a therapist.

A healthy boundary sounds like "I am going to take a break from dating."

Control sounds like "You need to stop dating because you are terrible at picking people."

Boundaries are not ways to control other people.

When People Won't Honor Your Boundaries

After you determine that certain people cannot or will not honor your boundary, the next course of action is to change your behavior in the relationship.

I've set the following boundary _____

_____ with _____,

and they refuse to honor my boundary. Since they have shown that they cannot/

will not honor my boundary, I will _____

_____ .

I've set the following boundary _____

_____ with _____,

and they refuse to honor my boundary. Since they have shown that they cannot/

will not honor my boundary, I will _____

_____

_____

_____ .

I've set the following boundary _____

_____ with _____,

and they refuse to honor my boundary. Since they have shown that they cannot/

will not honor my boundary, I will _____

_____

_____

_____ .

I've set the following boundary _____

_____ with _____ ,

and they refuse to honor my boundary. Since they have shown that they cannot/

will not honor my boundary, I will _____

_____

_____

_____

_____ .

Consequences

Consequences are not punitive; they're a way to protect yourself and enforce your boundaries with others. Allowing people to violate a limit repeatedly without effect is a way that you dishonor your own boundaries.

In the following scenarios, consider a consequence for the boundary violation:

1. You've asked your friend to stop bringing up your ex because you're trying to move on.

    What is the consequence for their refusal to adhere to this boundary?

_____

_____

_____

_____

2. Your brother borrowed $500 for his rent. He's always late paying you back, so this time you stressed the importance of returning the money on time. Nevertheless, he's late again.

What is the consequence for his refusal to adhere to this boundary?

3. You've asked your in-laws to respect your dietary choices for your kids. Yet they continue giving the children foods on your no-no list.

What is the consequence for their refusal to adhere to this boundary?

Pause: Sometimes, doing your part is the hardest part. Admitting that you're the person standing in your own way can be difficult and yet also freeing. Take a moment to admire how powerful you are.

Important Reminder: Sometimes it's best to leave before you reach your breaking point. It's okay to pivot without suffering for a prolonged period. Staying until you can't take any more takes a lot out of you. Enough can be enough, at your discretion.

Accepting Boundaries from Others

As you become more comfortable with placing boundaries, you may notice that you sometimes violate boundaries that others have set with you. There's no denying that it feels personal when someone sets limitations with you.

You may have experienced someone asking for space in a relationship, asking you to be on time, or making other requests based on their needs and expectations. As you've learned throughout this book, implementing boundaries isn't easy or effortless, so when someone places a boundary with you, know that they probably thought about it a lot (even if their delivery wasn't the best).

When _____ placed the following boundary with me _____

_____

_____ ,

I felt [use one word to describe your feelings] _____ .

When _____ placed the following boundary with me _____

_____

_____ ,

I felt [use one word to describe your feelings] _____ .

When _____ placed the following boundary with me _____

_____

_____ ,

I felt [use one word to describe your feelings] _____ .

When _____ placed the following boundary with me _____

_____

_____ ,

I felt [use one word to describe your feelings] _____ .

It's true that being on the receiving end of boundaries isn't always easy, but it's an important way to honor the needs of others.

Make a list of ways to care for yourself when boundaries are placed with you.

_____

_____

_____

_____

_____

_____

_____

How Culture Impacts the Ability to Set and Stick to Boundaries

My very first client was from an enmeshed family. My client wanted to be more autonomous, but in his culture, along with his mother, his older sister acted like a mother figure and took care of him. Unfortunately, this behavior blurred the lines between having siblings and having parents. He had to answer not only to his parents but also to his sister.

Sometimes, cultural norms can get in the way of establishing an identity for yourself. By developing your boundaries, you can become the person you want to be despite these norms.

In some cultures, boundary violations such as enmeshment are not seen as such because they're the norm. They become boundary violations when one person wants something different. In Black culture, it's widely accepted that you *cannot* talk back to adults. For myself and many of my peers, this cultural norm has left little room for individuality, openness, and comfort in our relationships with our elders.

Culture can be religious, geographical, ethnic, race-related, or environmental.

How has your culture of origin impacted your boundaries?

_____

_____

_____

_____

What boundaries do you have or want to have that are outside your culture's norms?

_____

_____

Gather Yourself

This chapter was about doing your part to honor yourself. Take a few minutes to appreciate all the things you are doing for your self-care.

10

All in the Family

When you want to set boundaries, family relationships are often the most challenging. Since your family knew you before you had a good understanding of yourself, your family's perception of you, as well as your perception of yourself, is partly based on ancient history. It can be scary to make changes to become more of who you really are. It's natural to fear how others may react to the "real" you.

How do you believe that you are perceived by your family of origin? For example, "My family believes that I have it all together because I rarely ask for support."

What do you wish they knew about you?

_____

_____

_____

_____

_____

Three Possible Reasons You May Find It Hard to Set Boundaries with Family

1. *You have no clue where to start.* For your entire life, you've lived with certain dynamics, and now that you're ready to change them, you aren't sure how to go about it.
2. *You feel certain that your family will reject your boundaries.* Sometimes, setting boundaries comes at the expense of further damaging unhealthy relationships.
3. *You feel like you're betraying your family's values.* Breaking away from the cultural norms in your family can feel like you're betraying them. But doing something for yourself is not against your family.

PARENTS JUST DON'T UNDERSTAND

The items below suggest that you need healthier boundaries with your parents. Mark off all areas that apply to you, and use the blank spaces to write some of your own specific examples.

❑ They are aware of intimate details of your romantic relationship (particularly if your parents are causing harm in the relationship).

- ❑ You feel pressured to act in a certain way to please them.
- ❑ They are involved in disputes you have with others.
- ❑ They don't respect your opinion.
- ❑ They enter your personal space without asking.
- ❑ They insist you say yes to everything.
- ❑ You say yes to them out of obligation, even when it's inconvenient.

❑ _____

❑ _____

❑ _____

Knowing Your Needs

Sometimes you might be unaware of what boundaries are needed and which boundaries you already have in place. For each of the following relationships, share a boundary that you have and one that you need.

I have the following boundaries with my mother:

_____

_____

_____

_____

_____

I need the following boundaries with my mother:

_____

_____

_____

_____

I have the following boundaries with my father:

_____

_____

_____

_____

I need the following boundaries with my father:

_____

_____

_____

_____

I have the following boundaries with my _____:

_____

_____

_____

_____

I need the following boundaries with my _____:

_____

_____

_____

_____

I have the following boundaries with my _____:

_____

_____

_____

_____

I need the following boundaries with my _____ :

_____

_____

_____

_____

_____

_____

Healthy Limits with Your Adult Children

Parenting is a lifetime job, but your role evolves from being 100 percent hands-on to being someone who plays a supportive role. When children become adults, parents need to transition to a new role.

The items below suggest that you need healthier boundaries with your adult child. Mark off all that apply to you.

❏ You help them make decisions in most areas of their lives.
❏ They are unable to care for themselves without your financial support.
❏ They lack key life skills, and you pick up the slack.
❏ They intrude on your time and space.
❏ They manipulate you into doing things for them.
❏ You feel taken advantage of in the relationship.

An important part of parenting adult children is providing them with resources, supporting them, and allowing them to create their own life.

I have the following boundaries with my adult children:

_____

_____

_____

_____

_____

I need the following boundaries with my adult children:

_____

_____

_____

_____

_____

Healthy Limits with Children Under Eighteen

Children benefit when parents have expectations of them. Clear and reasonable limitations help them feel loved and keep them safe. Although kids can be allotted some autonomy in their lives, it's essential to continue monitoring them and providing structure.

The items below suggest that you need healthier boundaries with your child. Mark off all areas that apply to you.

- They have no rules.
- Your parenting style is permissive.
- Your children are used as confidants.
- Your parenting style is punitive only.
- They are allowed to speak to others inappropriately.

I have the following boundaries with my children:

_____

_____

_____

_____

_____

I need the following boundaries with my children:

_____

_____

_____

_____

_____

Before I became a therapist, I was a juvenile probation officer. In my role, I serviced kids who were in placement (jail) and those in the community. When kids were sent to placement, I saw the majority of them change from criminals to teenagers. Much of the job with juveniles is centered on working with their families. Many of the children I served came from family environments with porous boundaries. The children didn't have structure, and being sent to placement gave them structure. Their schoolwork improved to grade level, they completed GED programs, and they improved their social skills.

Children need healthy boundaries in the home to be healthy people. They are not capable of managing themselves.

Write a letter to your younger self describing how different boundaries would've been helpful, or how the ones you had hurt or harmed you.

Healthy Limits with In-Laws

Issues with in-laws are often the result of poorly defined boundaries. Every family has its own way of relating. As you join into a family, your expectations are unknown to them. So it's vital to join with clear boundaries in place. In-laws have no prior knowledge of your needs, so they won't respect unstated boundaries—no one can.

When you pretend not to have any boundaries or wait for your partner to set them, you will suffer in your relationship with your in-laws. You can be kind and place boundaries with them respectfully.

The items below suggest that you need healthier boundaries with your in-laws. Mark off all areas that apply to you.

- ❏ They make your special family events (such as a wedding) about them.
- ❏ They gossip about you with their other family members.
- ❏ They don't like you and have told you as much.
- ❏ They openly share their negative views about you with your children.
- ❏ They question your parenting style.
- ❏ They make decisions for your family.
- ❏ They encourage your spouse or kids to keep secrets from you.
- ❏ They hear essential things happening with your partner before you hear about them.
- ❏ They give you gifts with strings attached.
- ❏ They give your kids things they know you wouldn't want them to have.
- ❏ They don't respect the way you parent your kids.

I have the following boundaries with my in-laws:

_____

_____

_____

_____

_____

I need the following boundaries with my in-laws:

_____

_____

_____

_____

_____

Other Family Members (Siblings, Grandparents, Cousins, etc.)

I have the following boundaries with _____:

_____

_____

_____

I need the following boundaries with _____:

I have the following boundaries with _____:

I need the following boundaries with _____:

Happy Holidays

As a relationship therapist, my practice gets busy around the holidays. It's the time of year when people become more anxious about finances and spend extended periods of time with family. The so-called most wonderful time of the year can be overwhelming when you don't practice healthy boundaries.

During the holiday season I struggle with:

Instead of existing as I have, this holiday season, I can:

_____

_____

_____

_____

_____

_____

Pause: Take a moment to stretch or breathe before moving on to the next activity.

Doing the Work

The only thing that makes setting boundaries easier is consistent practice. In this next exercise, fill in the blank, and answer the questions before and after setting boundaries.

Before

What is your biggest challenge in setting boundaries with your _____?

_____

_____

_____

_____

What boundaries does _____ have with you?

_____

_____

_____

_____

What boundary would you like your _____ to honor?

_____

_____

_____

_____

What will you say or do to execute your boundary?

_____

_____

_____

_____

What are the consequences if the boundary is not honored?

_____

_____

_____

_____

After

How did you feel setting the boundary?

_____

_____

_____

_____

If you feel any discomfort, how will you tend to it?

_____

_____

_____

_____

More Practice
Before

What is your biggest challenge setting boundaries with your _____?

_____

What boundaries does _____ have with you?

What boundary would you like your _____ to honor?

What will you say or do to execute your boundary?

What are the consequences if the boundary is not honored?

_____

_____

_____

_____

After

How did you feel setting the boundary?

_____

_____

_____

_____

If you feel any discomfort, how will you tend to it?

_____

_____

_____

_____

_____

And More Practice

Before

What is your biggest challenge setting boundaries with your _____ ?

_____

_____

_____

_____

What boundaries does _____ have with you?

_____

_____

_____

_____

What boundary would you like your _____ to honor?

_____

_____

_____

_____

What will you say or do to execute your boundary?

_____

_____

_____

_____

What are the consequences if the boundary is not honored?

_____

_____

_____

_____

After

How did you feel setting the boundary?

_____

_____

_____

_____

If you feel any discomfort, how will you tend to it?

_____

_____

_____

_____

Gather Yourself

Talking about family is often not easy. After completing this chapter, engage in a restorative self-care practice.

What came up for you while going through this chapter?

_____

_____

_____

_____

_____

_____

_____

_____

11

You Are Choosing Your Life When You Choose a Partner

Romantic Relationships

We create healthy romantic partnerships when we allow each other to grow, shift, and feel safe and honored. Relationships that seem perfect are the result of doing the work.

CHECKING IN

Select the boxes below that are true for your current romantic relationship:

❏ Your commitment to each other is clear.
❏ You and your partner compromise to make things work.
❏ You can communicate your needs and opinions.
❏ You feel safe physically.
❏ You support each other.
❏ You feel safe being yourself.
❏ You can respectfully disagree.
❏ You speak kindly to each other.
❏ Your growth is not a threat to the relationship.
❏ You're able to grow together.

In a romantic relationship, partners make agreements with each other. Sometimes, those agreements are explicitly stated: "I will cook dinner four or five times a week." Other times, the agreements are implicit, such as not typically making any attempts to cook dinner.

Using the space below, list the explicit and implicit agreements in your relationship.

Explicit agreements:

_____

_____

_____

_____

Implicit agreements:

_____

_____

_____

_____

Even if you've never spoken up for yourself in your relationship, you can start today.

What are your top three unmet needs you'd like to express to your partner?

Is your partner aware of these needs?

What can you say or do to make your needs clear to your partner?

Partnering with someone is one of the most important decisions we make in life. The person you decide to spend your life with can impact your finances, relationships with others, mental health, and overall quality of life. In choosing a partner, you are choosing your quality of life.

Pay Attention to the Signs

Green Flags

Positive indicators that demonstrate healthy qualities, such as being a good listener or showing a willingness to understand an opposing perspective.

Yellow Flags

Potential areas of concern that have not reached their peak but certainly cause worry. Example: The person you're dating doesn't have any friends and speaks about most relationships in a disparaging way.

Red Flags

If someone is harmful to others or to themselves, liking them isn't a reason to continue a romantic relationship with them. Clear indications of danger should never be ignored, as red flags tend to plague relationships long-term. Example: You're dating someone with significant financial issues who always asks to borrow money without paying it back.

In the following exercise, respond to the prompts about your current romantic relationship or a relationship from the past.

Name the green flags:

_____

_____

_____

_____

Name the yellow flags:

_____

_____

_____

_____

Name the red flags:

_____

_____

_____

_____

You Cannot Change People

Rather than dating someone you want to change, it's best to date the type of person you truly want to be with in a relationship. In my years of working with couples, I've seen that one thing is for sure: Over time, people become more themselves in relationships. If there's something that bothers you, set your expectations early and realistically.

Important Reminder: Sometimes you have to accept people or situations as they are without changing them. Acceptance is not an easy process, but neither is resisting the truth. It can be hard to accept things that you wish would change. But admitting what you can and can't control is best for your mental health. Acceptance allows you to stop struggling, but it doesn't mean that you are giving up hope.

Repeat Yourself

You will have to repeat yourself to get what you want. In many cases, your partner won't remember every request you've made. Asking them to honor your boundaries is similar to asking them to practice a new habit. It's a process to learn and apply new information consistently.

Repeating myself makes me feel _____ .
For my partner to hear me, I will repeat the following boundary:

_____

_____

_____

Once I've repeated my boundaries several times, if they're still dishonored, I can do or say the following:

_____

_____

_____

_____

Setting Expectations in Relationships

Sometimes, we learn our needs by knowing what is and isn't working. It's okay if your expectations in the relationship are different from what others may want or need in their relationships. For instance, you may enjoy sleeping in a separate bedroom from your snoring partner. This arrangement might not work for other couples, but if it works for you, continue with it.

Make a list of what's working in your relationship.

_____

_____

_____

_____

_____

_____

Make a list of what you would like to improve in your relationship.

_____

_____

_____

_____

_____

_____

_____

Pause: Who is your boundary hero? Think of a person in your life who reflects the type of boundaries that you would like to express and maintain.

Humans Are Imperfect

You are human. You aren't perfect, and neither is your partner. When you make requests of others, you're asking them to change *their* habits. Take a moment to consider how challenging it is to change your habits, even when you want to do it.

I found it challenging to change the following habits:

Example: Greeting my partner when they arrived home for work was a difficult adjustment for me.

I still have a hard time changing the following habits:

    Example: My partner constantly reminds me to put my phone away while
    we're talking.

When my partner has a difficult time remembering my boundaries, I can remind myself of the following:

Example: Changing habits isn't easy.

Talking About Solutions

In relationships, it's quite common to talk about problems as if there weren't a solution. Talking about the solution is a way to minimize the drama and move forward. In truth, you often know the solution, and waiting for the other person to guess what it is won't help you get your point across. Let's practice talking about the solution in a few common relationship situations.

Scenario:

Your partner tells you what to do instead of listening to you vent.

Solution:

"I want you to listen instead of telling me what to do. I just need to get my frustrations out."

Scenario:

Your partner took money from the joint savings account without talking to you about the withdrawal.

Solution:

_____

_____

_____

_____

Scenario:

You are tired of planning the vacations for the family all by yourself.

Solution:

_____

_____

_____

_____

We Learn from Example

What did you learn about romantic relationships from your parents?

_____

_____

_____

_____

_____

_____

What do you want to do differently from what you witnessed with your parents?

_____

_____

_____

_____

_____

Gather Yourself

We're all human and flawed. As humans, we don't always get things right, but we can evolve into better versions of ourselves.

What came up for you while going through this chapter?

12

The Family We Choose (Friends)

Friends are the family we choose for ourselves.
—EDNA BUCHANAN

Friendships are sacred relationships that we choose to have with others. Outside of family, they're the hardest relationships for us to implement boundaries in. Sometimes, a friend might share a troubling experience they had with someone else, which gives you a clue about how they would respond to your boundaries. That can make you second-guess the safety of expressing your needs.

Over time, we become keenly aware of how our friends are likely to respond to or feel about boundaries, and sometimes, we recognize the unhealthy parts of ourselves in them.

To help you sort through your thoughts and feelings about placing boundaries with a friend, complete the following statements:

My friend _____ seems to have an issue when people _____

_____. This makes me feel

_____

_____ about placing boundaries with them.

My friend _____ seems to have an issue when people _____

_____. This makes me feel

_____ about placing boundaries with them.

My friend _____ seems to have an issue when people _____

_____. This makes me feel

_____ about placing boundaries with them.

My friend _____ seems to have an issue when people _____

_____. This makes me feel

_____ about placing boundaries with them.

The average friendship lasts about seven years. Three things happen that impact our ability to maintain friendships:

1. As we evolve, we change. Therefore, our friendships may no longer fit our current needs. It's natural to transition from who we were, yet it can be hard to accept that friendships don't always grow with us.
2. As we get older, we find it more challenging to dedicate time to friendships. As children, we're able to be in the moment with others. As adults, we find that it becomes increasingly hard to balance our friendships with our family life, work life, and other demands.
3. Childhood friendships are primarily based on proximity and shared interests. Children play with one another without knowing much about someone's personality. Adult relationships are formed around connection,

personality, values, shared interests, and other factors. Therefore, finding "our people" becomes slightly more complicated.

The critical part of maintaining friendships is continuing to nurture healthy ones. If you've lost touch with someone, reach out to them. If you want to create new friendships, consider the people you already have in your life, such as coworkers and acquaintances, and work toward deepening those connections.

LIST YOUR FRIENDSHIPS THAT HAVE LASTED LONGER THAN SEVEN YEARS.	LIST FRIENDSHIPS THAT YOU'VE BUILT WITHIN THE PAST FIVE YEARS.

On the checklists below, mark each response that resonates with you.

SIGNS OF A HEALTHY FRIENDSHIP
- ❏ Your friend wants to see you grow.
- ❏ The friendship is mutually supportive.
- ❏ The friendship is mutually beneficial.
- ❏ Your friendship evolves as you evolve.
- ❏ You understand how to support each other.
- ❏ Setting boundaries doesn't threaten the friendship.
- ❏ Your friend is happy for you to be yourself.
- ❏ Your friend acknowledges your quirks and works around them.
- ❏ You can talk to your friend about your feelings.

SIGNS OF AN UNHEALTHY FRIENDSHIP

- ❏ The relationship is competitive.
- ❏ You exhibit your worst behavior when you're with your friend.
- ❏ You feel emotionally drained after connecting with your friend.
- ❏ Your friend tries to embarrass you in front of others.
- ❏ You don't have anything in common.
- ❏ Your friend shares details of your personal life with others.
- ❏ The friendship is not reciprocal (i.e., you give more than you receive).
- ❏ You're unable to work through disagreements.
- ❏ Your friend doesn't respect your boundaries.
- ❏ The relationship is enmeshed or codependent.

Using the checklists above, which of your friendships meet the criteria for healthy friendships, and which meet the criteria for unhealthy friendships? List them below:

_____

_____

_____

_____

Common Issues in Friendships

Complaining

Many of us need someone to talk to, but we can't always be that person for those who deplete our energy and impact our mental health. Remember that your needs matter, too, and you deserve to have mutually supportive conversations. It's okay to redirect the conversation, minimize talk time, and not respond when it isn't a good time for you.

While talking about problems is cathartic, listening to someone talk about their problems regularly can be draining. Complaining falls into one of three categories: venting, problem-solving, or ruminating. Venting is a way to talk about issues without seeking guidance, but rather to simply let out our frustrations. Problem-solving is seeking guidance or advice on how to correct an issue. Ruminating is talking about the same issues over and over without trying to problem-solve or work through our frustrations in any real way.

When your friend is a chronic complainer, what can you say to shift the conversation?

1.

2.

3.

4.

5.

6.

Being the Therapist in the Relationship

You may be great at giving sound advice, but if you're tired, you can stop.

List seven things you can do instead of offering advice and feedback. Hint: Just listening can be one of the best ways to support someone.

Helping someone without offering solutions sounds like this:

- "I hear you. How can I support you?"
- "Thank you for trusting me with that."
- "Please tell me what you need from me."

- "I'm listening."
- "Cry, and feel what you need to."
- "Thank you for sharing with me."
- "I love you, and I'm here for you."
- "I don't have an answer, but I'm here to listen."

Differences of Opinion

The beautiful thing about communication is that you can decide how you respond. In any relationship, you won't always agree with the other person. Instead of talking about hot-button topics, focus the conversation on areas that allow you to enjoy your time together.

Complete the following statements.

With _____ , I enjoy talking about

_____ .

With them, I don't enjoy talking about _____ .

_____ .

With _____ , I enjoy talking about

_____ .

With them, I don't enjoy talking about _____ .

_____ .

With _____ , I enjoy talking about

_____ .

With them, I don't enjoy talking about _____ .

_____ .

With _____ , I enjoy talking about

_____ .

With them, I don't enjoy talking about _____ .

_____ .

With _____, I enjoy talking about

_____ .

With them, I don't enjoy talking about_____ .

_____ .

With _____, I enjoy talking about

_____ .

With them, I don't enjoy talking about _____ .

_____ .

Remember, you don't have to talk about everything with everyone, and you don't have to listen to a friend's opinion on every topic.

Examples:

"I'm not looking for feedback, I just want to vent."

"I'm already sure of what I want to do in this situation."

"I'm not ready to share more at this time."

Important Reminder: Not everyone gives sound advice. Some advice is biased. Some advice is rooted in fear. Some advice comes from people who don't have the tools to help you. When seeking advice, consider who you're talking to and if their perspective is for you. Seek wise counsel.

Pause: Take a moment to think about what type of friend you are to others.

Addressing Issues as They Arise

In any relationship, the best time to address issues is in the moment. Sometimes you may not notice that you have an issue with something, but it's best to address it as soon as you realize it. If you ruminate and wait until the perfect time, you'll likely express your boundary in an aggressive or passive-aggressive manner. Let's practice addressing boundary violations right away.

You planned a lunch with your friends outdoors. The restaurant has a ten-minute window for holding reservations, and one of your friends has a history of being late.

What will you say or do?

_____

_____

_____

_____

Your friend constantly solicits your advice on her marriage. You feel uncomfortable telling her what's best. As you're talking to her, she says, "I'm considering separating from my partner."

What will you say or do?

_____

_____

_____

_____

You find out your friend is sharing your business with other mutual friends. What will you say or do?

_____

_____

_____

_____

Reasons People Stay in Unhealthy Friendships

Longevity

Sometimes you've been friends with someone for so long that you learn to tolerate and accommodate unhealthy behaviors. Carrying on friendships or any relationship beyond its expiration date typically leaves you feeling depleted and resentful. It's understandable that you'd want to maintain friendships with the people who've known you since middle school, but consider if those connections are unhealthy.

Going Through a Rough Patch

Lots of people go through things in their personal lives that impact their friendships. When this is the case, hopefully it's temporary. When it's prolonged, however, it might not be just a rough patch. It could be an indication that the friendship isn't healthy for you.

Staying for Hope

Hoping someone will change is not a good reason for staying in an unhealthy relationship.

Waiting for Something Big to Happen

Although the relationship is unhealthy, you might be waiting for something big to happen in order to gather the courage to end it.

Fear of Dealing with the Discomfort

The fear of the fallout if you leave the friendship may seem like an insurmountable barrier to change. It's undoubtedly sad when relationships end, but it may be the best thing for you. Leaving a relationship takes consideration and clarity.

In the past, I've stayed in unhealthy friendships because:

_____

_____

_____

_____

_____

_____

Presently, I'm choosing to remain in unhealthy friendships because:

_____

_____

_____

_____

_____

_____

_____

_____

_____

Important Reminder: Breaking up with a friend may hurt even when it is the best thing for you. Allow yourself to grieve the loss of the friendship. You can move forward without forgetting about the relationship. Friendships are deep connections, and it makes sense to be deeply impacted when a friendship ends.

A few reminders about friendships:
- As you shift, so will your friendships.
- It's okay to outgrow people.
- At different points in life, you will need different things from different people.
- Frenemies are not friends.
- You can, but you are not obligated to, tell your friends everything.
- You can't keep a friendship together on your own.

WHAT DO YOU NEED?

What boundaries would you like to have in your friendships? Which boundaries do you need to refresh, and which do you need to be more consistent about?

I have the following boundaries with _____:

_____

_____

_____

_____

I need the following boundaries with _____:

_____

_____

_____

_____

I have the following boundaries with _____:

_____

_____

_____

_____

I need the following boundaries with _____ :

I have the following boundaries with _____ :

I need the following boundaries with _____ :

Gather Yourself

You choose your friends, and you can choose to improve your relationships for your well-being and peace of mind.

What came up for you while going through this chapter?

13

WORKing on Your Boundaries

The average full-time employee works forty-plus hours a week. That's more time than you spend in any other setting, so how you function in the work space is critical.

WORK ASSESSMENT

Place a check mark next to each area that you struggle with at work:

- ❑ Doing work for others
- ❑ Being asked about personal issues
- ❑ Taking on more than you can handle
- ❑ Not delegating
- ❑ Flirting
- ❑ Working without pay
- ❑ Not taking advantage of vacation days
- ❑ Saying yes to tasks you can't responsibly complete
- ❑ Engaging in stressful interactions
- ❑ Working during downtime
- ❑ Doing jobs intended for more than one person
- ❑ Not taking needed time off

For each of the areas you selected, name one needed boundary. Remember to frame your boundaries with "I need," "I expect," or "I want."

Likes and Dislikes

Every job has aspects you love and aspects you'd rather do without. I love my job as a therapist, but I don't like certain administrative tasks like billing. Even though I don't like these tasks, they're essential if I want to be paid for the parts of the job I do love.

List the areas of your job that you like:

List the areas of your job that you do not like:

For each of the areas that you don't like, use the chart below to consider how to manage those tasks.

TASK	CAN THIS TASK BE ELIMINATED OR SIMPLIFIED? YES OR NO	CAN I ASK FOR HELP? YES OR NO	CAN I DELEGATE THIS? YES OR NO	IS THERE AN EASIER WAY TO COMPLETE THIS TASK? YES OR NO	WHAT'S THE EASIEST SOLUTION?	IS IT POSSIBLE TO PAIR THIS TASK WITH SOMETHING I ENJOY? EXAMPLE: LISTENING TO MUSIC WHILE COMPLETING MONTHLY REPORTS

Reframe the Way You View the Situation

Reframing is a technique that allows you to shift your mindset from something negative to something positive and, therefore, more helpful. It helps you put things into perspective when you can't change a situation.

Example: My boss will *never* let me have the time off I requested.
Reframe: The company has a policy that allows me to take time off as long as I request it in advance.

Using the space below, practice reframing some of your "always" and "never" thoughts about work.

_____

_____

_____

_____

_____

_____

_____

_____

_____

_____

Handling a Toxic Work Environment

You can't choose your coworkers, but you can choose how you respond to them. For example, how can you handle the following workplace situations?

When people are gossiping in the office, I can:

_____

_____

When it's requested that I work long hours, I can:

When cliques are formed at work, I can:

When I'm assigned more work on top of my already overwhelming
workload, I can:

When I have issues with my boss, I can:

_____

_____

_____

_____

When I have issues with my coworker, I can:

_____

_____

_____

_____

If I experience sexual harassment, bullying, or mistreatment based on race, physical ability, or sexual orientation, I can:

_____

_____

_____

_____

Pause: Take a moment to pause and reflect on the times when you've felt happy at work. What was happening during those times?

Hire Well

You can't change people, but you can change yourself. If you're in the position to hire people, make sure that you hire those who are capable of doing the job. Sometimes you hire people because they're nice, because they were recommended, or because you may simply like them. But it's important that they're able to complete their job duties.

I've made the following mistakes when hiring people:

_____

_____

_____

_____

_____

_____

_____

If you've made mistakes in the past, commit to do better next time. Don't merely hope that things will turn out differently if you make the same mistake again.

How to Set Boundaries at Work

1. Identify the areas where boundaries are needed with _____.
   You can uncover these by tuning in to your feelings. For example, if you
   are staying later than you'd like, what's causing this behavior on your part?
   What about your job leads you to feel overwhelmed or burned out?

   _____

   _____

   _____

   _____

2. If at all possible, do your work only during work hours. Particularly when
   working from home, try to stick to your work and avoid distractions. If
   you need to do something personal, take a planned break away for a set
   amount of time.

3. Give yourself permission to create boundaries in all areas of your life,
   including work. If you hold back from expressing what you need, you will
   feel resentment toward your coworkers and employer.

4. Don't let issues go too far before you decide to set boundaries. Start setting
   them right at the onset of the problem.

5. Teach others how to respect your boundaries by being consistent about
   respecting them yourself. If you choose to declare your expectations, be
   clear and up-front.

Setting Boundaries with Your Boss

Sometimes, bosses have personalities that don't make it easy to set boundaries. Also, you may not know how to clearly articulate your needs. And of course, there's a fear of coming off as rude and causing damage to your relationship with your boss.

Let's practice language around setting boundaries with your boss. Remember to be clear, concise, and consistent.

Examples:

"I need help with my workload because I can't manage everything on my plate."

"I don't feel comfortable talking about politics at work."

Write three of your own using the space below:

1.

2.

3.

_____

_____

_____

_____

Managing Burnout

Burnout is the result of doing too much, feeling underappreciated, having un-reasonable expectations, or participating in activities that provide you with little value. Certain unpleasant tasks or interactions may be a part of the job, but in some cases, burnout can be prevented.

I do more than required in the following areas:

_____

_____

_____

_____

_____

I feel underappreciated when:

_____

_____

I set the following unreasonable expectations:

I receive little value from the following:

To prevent myself from getting burned out, I can:

_____

_____

_____

_____

If I'm having a challenging day at work, I can:

_____

_____

_____

_____

_____

Off-Hours

Sometimes you disrespect your own boundaries by working during off-hours or while on vacation. When you feel the need to work after hours, ask yourself, "Is this urgent?" There's a difference between urgent, important, and work that can wait. Describe the difference between these three areas.

What's urgent?

_____

_____

_____

What's important?

_____

_____

_____

What can wait?

_____

_____

_____

The Art of Unplugging

There's always work to be done. Know when to leave tasks for the next day.

What do you enjoy doing with your time outside of work?

_____

_____

What hobbies would you like to explore?

What activities make you feel most like yourself?

How do you want to be remembered?

Gather Yourself

What if we stopped celebrating being busy as a measurement of importance?
What if instead we celebrated how much time we had spent listening,
pondering, meditating, and enjoying time with the most important people in
our lives?

—GREG MCKEOWN

What came up for you while going through this chapter?

14

Social Media and Technology

Because we live in a digital world, technology is a massive part of how we function. Even with technology all around us, we can curate a healthy digital experience.

ASSESSMENT OF SOCIAL MEDIA BOUNDARIES

Using the checklist below, mark each area where you struggle with healthy boundaries.

- ❏ You find yourself constantly checking your phone when you're supposed to focus on something else.
- ❏ You spend excessive amounts of time on your phone. The average person spends about three hours a day on their phone.
- ❏ In social settings, you're glued to your phone instead of socializing.
- ❏ You regularly use your phone as an escape from working, parenting, completing tasks, or being present with others.
- ❏ People have complained about your digital usage.
- ❏ You use your phone while driving.
- ❏ Your technology usage impacts your ability to function in other areas, such as in school, at work, or at home.
- ❏ Your technology usage hurts your mental or emotional health.

The positive attention that many people receive keeps them posting and wanting more. It's true that social media can be hard to break away from. With each like and view, your brain receives a hit of dopamine that keeps you wanting more. And sometimes, to receive the admiration that some find on social media, you may find yourself becoming a different version of yourself.

What do you portray on social media? What might people assume about you based solely on what you post and share?

_____

_____

_____

_____

_____

When you see something on social media that causes you discomfort, what can you say to reassure yourself?

_____

_____

_____

_____

Is there an action that you need to take to ease your discomfort? If so, what is that action?

The Good and Bad of Technology

I cannot imagine a world without TV. As a child, I slept with a TV in my bedroom, and through most of college I continued this practice. It wasn't until my TV broke during my senior year of undergraduate that I considered watching less TV. By necessity, at least for a few weeks, I lived without a TV. Not only did I survive, but I broke my habit of sleeping with the television in my bedroom. I found my sleep to be more restful without it, and I no longer spent time lingering in bed when I needed to get my day started. Watching television is still one of my favorite pastimes. However, I'm more intentional with when and what I watch.

What are some good aspects of technology?

Example: Being able to FaceTime parents who live in another state.

_____

_____

_____

_____

_____

_____

What are some bad aspects of technology?

Example: Seeing your friends having fun without you on social media.

_____

_____

_____

_____

_____

_____

Social Media Isn't the Only Cure for Boredom

Oftentimes, scrolling on social media is done out of boredom. Make a list of things that you'd rather do than use social media.

Your Energy Is a Reflection of What You Consume

Have you ever been feeling fine and then you happen upon something that completely changed your mood? Whether it's watching the news or who you follow on social media, you can determine what is and isn't working and make changes as needed.

Who or what types of accounts do you enjoy following on social media?

Who or what accounts cause your mood to shift in a negative way?

_____

_____

_____

_____

_____

Pause: Take a moment to remember when social media wasn't a daily part of your life.

Fear of Missing Out (FOMO)

You will not be included in everything. And you will not include everyone in every aspect of your life. It makes sense that we can feel upset when excluded from gatherings and other experiences we see on social media.

When you are feeling left out, what can you say to reassure yourself?

1.

_____

_____

_____

2.

3.

4.

5.

Reasons to unfollow people on social media:

- They post too often (for your liking).
- You feel annoyed, frustrated, or angry by their posts.
- Their posts aren't relevant to you.
- You find yourself complaining about their content.
- You often feel inferior (not enough).
- The content is not consistent with who you are.
- You don't like what they represent.
- You find yourself comparing your life with the lives of the people you follow.

Strategies to Minimize Digital Overload
Social Media Cleanse
There are two ways to do a digital cleanse.

Option 1
Restrict yourself from using social media by removing yourself from it completely for a certain amount of time.

What length of time will I commit to not using social media?

What habits do I need to change to honor my commitment?
    Example: Remove the app from your phone.

How will I ease my way back into social media?

_____

_____

_____

How do I want to use social media differently long-term?

_____

_____

_____

Option 2

Manage the way you show up.

In this exercise, I want you to go through the list of people you follow. For each account, consider how you feel connected or disconnected from their content. If you feel disconnected, exercise your power to mute or unfollow.

How much time do you want to spend on social media?

_____

_____

How much time do you want to spend on other areas of technology such as watching TV or the news?

Are there certain times of the day that you want to spend technology-free? If so, when or during what activities?

Could removing some apps from your phone be helpful? If so, which apps?

Gather Yourself

What came up for you while going through this chapter?

Final Note

There is no easy way to do hard things. The practice of setting healthy boundaries is ongoing. Just as you begin to manage one area, you may find yourself needing healthy boundaries in another area. It's okay to pause when needed to revisit the work of understanding boundaries. Use this book as a resource throughout your practice. Revisit the various sections as needed, and remember to take the time to pause and reflect when this work feels challenging. It isn't easy, but it's worth the effort.

After completing this book, what have you learned about yourself?

_____

_____

_____

_____

_____

_____

_____

_____

_____

_____

_____

_____

Take this space to write a few affirmations to refer to when you need reassurance around setting boundaries. For example, "I have healthy boundaries at work," and "I can maintain healthy boundaries with my mother."

_____

_____

_____

_____

_____

_____

Take this space to envision what your life would be like with healthier boundaries.

_____

_____

_____

_____

_____

_____

_____

_____

_____

_____

Complete this sentence: I am becoming _____.

_____

_____

_____

_____

Additional Reading

There are many books that have helped me understand and implement healthy boundaries in my own life, as well as in my work with clients. A few key references are listed below.

CHAPTER 4

Farnsworth, Bryn. "How to Measure Emotions and Feelings (and the Difference Between Them)." iMotions. https://imotions.com/blog/difference-feelings-emotions (accessed May 18, 2021).

Taylor, Jill Bolte. *My Stroke of Insight: A Brain Scientist's Personal Journey.* New York: Viking, 2006.

CHAPTER 13

Maxwell, John C. *Failing Forward: Turning Mistakes into Stepping Stones for Success.* BookBaby, 2014.

———. *The 21 Irrefutable Laws of Leadership: Follow Them and People Will Follow You.* Nashville, TN: Thomas Nelson, 2008.

CHAPTER 14

McKeown, Greg. *Essentialism: The Disciplined Pursuit of Less.* London: Virgin Books, 2021.

About the Author

Photograph of the author © Ariel Perry

Nedra Glover Tawwab, MSW, LCSW, is the author of the *New York Times* bestseller *Set Boundaries, Find Peace.* A licensed therapist and renowned relationship expert, she has practiced relationship therapy for fourteen years and is the founder and owner of the group therapy practice Kaleidoscope Counseling. She has been recently featured in *The New York Times*, *The Guardian*, *Psychology Today*, *Self*, and *Vice*, and has appeared on numerous podcasts, including *Sofia with an F*, *The School of Greatness*, and *Therapy for Black Girls*. Tawwab runs a popular Instagram account where she shares practices, tools, and reflections for mental health and hosts weekly Q&As about boundaries and relationships. She lives in North Carolina with her family.

ALSO BY
NEDRA GLOVER TAWWAB

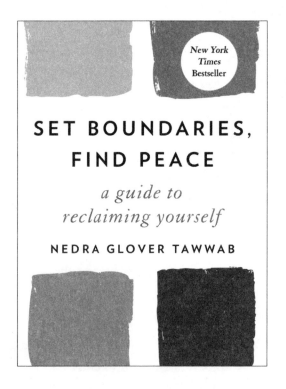